The Picnic Cookbook

The Picnic Cookbook

Laura Mason

National Trust

First published in the United Kingdom in 2015 by
National Trust Books
1 Gower Street
London WC1E 6HD

An imprint of Pavilion Books Group

ISBN: 9781909881396

A CIP catalogue record for this book is available from the British Library.

10 9 8 7 6 5 4 3 2 1

Reproduction by Mission Productions, Hong Kong
Printed by Toppan Leefung, China

This book can be ordered direct from the publisher
at the website: www.pavilionbooks.com, or try your local bookshop.
Also available at National Trust shops or www.shop.nationaltrust.org.uk.

All photographs by Yuki Sugiura, other than:

National Trust Images/Joe Cornish: p.82; NTI/Paul Harris: p.188; NTI /David Levenson:
p.74; NTI /John Millar: p98, p.104; NTI /John Miller: p.160; NTI/Robert Morris: p.180;
NTI /Navid Noton: p.168.
Alamy/Cristian Gusa: p.108

Contents

Outdoors

Eating outdoors, be it a picnic, a barbecue or a campfire fry-up, brings out an optimistic streak in the British. Appetites will be sharpened by the fresh air and there is an opportunity to lounge on the grass or seashore, to admire a wonderful view, or to feel a sense of freedom. English literature is full of these events both real and imagined. Sometimes it might be admitted that conditions were less than ideal, and the weather is frequently blamed – as if everyone imagined that the usual changeable climate might behave itself simply because someone had arranged an outdoor party.

What an attraction the picnic has for us, what a hold on our imagination. All the elements that feed into our ideas of the event can be seen in the tangled strands of its history. The word, of mysterious origin, arrived in the English language in the late 18th century and quickly came to mean a pleasure excursion including an outdoor meal, often one to which each person made a contribution by providing some food.

There were precedents for eating outside: hunting parties and informal collations taken in special banqueting houses, set on the roofs of mansions or at special viewpoints in the grounds of large houses. But at about this time, the Romantic movement also brought new ideas about the joys of being outdoors, especially in rugged scenery. William and Dorothy Wordsworth and their circle were notable picnickers.

However much food we might pack into the boot of the car, we are amateurs compared to the Victorians. Mrs Beeton's *Book of Household Management* (1861) provided a menu, surely idealised, for a picnic for 40 people. Large quantities of cold cuts and meat pies, lobsters, baskets full of salad, jar upon jar of stewed fruit, pastry of various descriptions, a large Christmas pudding ('this must be good'), fruit, cheese and the wherewithal for tea – bread, butter and three types of cake – are all listed. Ale, ginger beer, soda water, lemonade, sherry, claret, champagne and brandy are suggested as beverages. The outdoors not only sharpens the appetite – it also sharpens the thirst.

The informality of eating outside still has great appeal, but it must have been appreciated much more in the past. James Tissot's painting *The Picnic* (1876) shows some of the joys of such an occasion. The young men and women of the party flirt in an urban setting, the garden of his own home in London, and there is cake, bread and butter, and a kettle is set on a spirit burner in the foreground. It is autumn, the horse chestnut leaves are golden and brown, and scarves, caps, rugs and shawls are all evident. The season, although late, is clearly no obstacle to frivolous enjoyment of food and company outdoors.

Left Find a picturesque picnic spot
and create your own unique dining space.

Further freedom, which we take for granted, came with the invention of the motor car. *Picnics for Motorists*, by Mrs Leyel, was published in 1936, with menus of mousses and galantines, jellied cold dishes, extravagant pies and meat dishes. 'Everything seemed to contain truffles', said the friend who lent her copy to me. This isn't true, but the book has the aura of a time when money was no particular object, and ladies of leisure, although they might have learnt their way around a kitchen, undoubtedly had someone to do the washing-up while they packed a basket of delicacies and drove off to meet friends at some beauty spot. Mrs Leyel was an advocate of the thermos flask, although many took a kettle along and made tea fresh as required.

Most importantly, a picnic is an escape, a break from routine. Ambrose Heath wrote of this in *Good Sandwiches and Picnic Dishes* (1948): 'For children it is an ineffable glance into Paradise, when the shackles of restraint are unloosed, and for far too brief a while realities withdraw.' He captures the curious tension, evident in all the best picnics: a mixture of spontaneity and good planning. The sense of time apart is emphasised again and again in descriptions of good picnics.

Ambrose Heath makes another very important point: it is best to agree a destination in advance, for if you set off with no particular place in mind, you may well find yourself 'shot out upon some unlovely roadside with no more than an unappetising row of modern brick cottages and a farmyard midden' – or these days, more likely, its modern equivalent, the car park of a motorway services.

The food and destination are within one's control, but picnics have many potential hazards – weather, wasps, stray animals. I've sat in the car drinking tea from a flask while heavy rain blurred a view of tarmac, and I've cowered behind a wall in a hailstorm, trying to eat disintegrating cake from frozen fingers. Elizabeth David described an unnerving experience during a picnic in India (the members of the British Raj were great picnickers), of eating while surrounded by a circle of stray dogs that howled in unison. Another intrusion into the bucolic ideal is shown in the late 19th-century painting, *The Pig's Picnic*, by William Weekes. A broad damask cloth is spread on the ground, elaborately set with cutlery and glasses. A stack of plates, bottles of champagne, a neatly garnished pie and a roast of beef await the company. The lone guardian of all this, a small boy, lies asleep, his shiny top hat discarded, while unobserved, a large black pig advances with a mixture of caution and curiosity across the snowy cloth towards a brilliant carmine lobster. Sometimes, one feels that lurking disaster is also part of the picnic mix, to be enjoyed retrospectively.

Provisions for travellers and food for walks have an element of necessity about them. They need to be easy to carry and easy to eat and to satisfy. There is the possibility of being tetchy and bored with carrying the picnic, but the probability of an appetite sharpened by an early start and chilly weather. Eating a meal outdoors is a product, not the object, of the day. But there is no reason why it should not be good and pleasurable, and a well-made sandwich from home cheers a long journey in a way that no pre-packed offering can. During my childhood there was a very clear division between taking a picnic for a day out and taking food because one was on a journey. It was nicer, and of course cheaper, to take food from home and not be at the mercy of cafés or railway-station buffets. That the food was usually egg sandwiches and a flask of tea, whatever the occasion, was beside the point.

In the English love affair with eating al fresco, the barbecue is a late arrival. It is noticeable that, although many authors from the past would have been familiar with the notion of spit-roasting and cooking on a grid-iron in the kitchen, the idea of carrying this into the outdoors is limited. Grand celebratory events such as ox-roasts aside, few people seem to have grilled their food outdoors (an exception being Sir Walter Scott, whose salmon-fishing expeditions to the Tweed often ended with cooking the catch). As with so much else to do with food, the idea arrived in the mid-20th century. The North American influence – burgers, steaks and a plethora of sauces – and foreign holidays, in which the British found themselves salivating at the smells of meat or fish grilled over charcoal on the shores of the Mediterranean, played a large part in the rise of the barbecue's popularity. It is difficult to imagine this as a novelty now, when every fine weekend seems to lead to the mass lighting of charcoal across the country, but a barbecue still captures that essential of eating outdoors, a space outside ordinary time, a bit of a party.

Campfire cookery was, and remains, a many and varied thing. The modern-day romantic is likely to be found practising bushcraft, regarding the woods as a kind of outdoor kitchen. Serious campers, intent on long-distance walks or bagging Munros, tend to believe in packaged food and gas-fired stoves, and, indeed, the old-fashioned campfire tends to be discouraged in many places. It was essential for the tramp of the past with a billycan, and for eccentrics like the writer and artist Dorothy Hartley who walked through the English countryside of the 1920s and 1930s. This kind of necessity is not desirable in outdoor food. Countrymen and women of the past, obliged to work outdoors and often to eat their modest midday meals there too, had reservations about eating outside for pleasure and retreated indoors.

Wealthy and leisured picnickers, on the other hand, would light a fire as part of an al fresco meal, sometimes just to boil a kettle, sometimes more. The Reverend Francis Kilvert described many picnics in his diary during the 19th century, one of which included a disastrous attempt to boil a pot of new potatoes over a campfire. My Aunty Nan, the queen of outdoor cooking in my family (and of outdoor food in general) was always ready to spend time under canvas. She and my Uncle Jack happily camped in the field adjacent to our farmhouse every May, even though they actually lived in a village only a mile away. They had many reasons for doing this, but much of the appeal seemed to be a campfire, daily breakfast fry-ups, and once again, that sense of space beyond routine.

Picnic Practicalities

Picnics can be as planned or impromptu as you like, but it is always useful to have thoughts about good places to go, and the items which make the meal easier, more comfortable or more elegant when one arrives.

Where to go?

First, choose your spot, whether it is a location that has long been a favourite with your family or somewhere new to explore. It could be your own back garden or the local park, a location where a special event is being hosted, or a remote spot in a national park or area of outstanding natural beauty that you have chosen on a whim. The chances are that most places will encourage visitors and often make some provision in the form of picnic tables and other facilities (not to mention cafés, if the weather really turns nasty), but always check access first.

National Trust properties include many superb locations for eating al fresco. The organisation looks after miles of coastline and acres of countryside in which to meet friends and share some good food. Many properties welcome picnics – some have a designated picnic area, although a few cannot accommodate them. Look out for the 'suitable for picnics' icon on the individual property's web pages. Use the property search at www.nationaltrust.org.uk to find a place to visit, or consider some of the options outlined below.

My own favourite is Fountains Abbey, near Ripon, where ancient woodland, the ruined abbey, 18th-century water gardens and glimpses of the estate's deer combine in a deeply tranquil landscape. Stowe in Buckinghamshire is another place with glorious views, created as an earthly paradise with lakeside walks and classical temples in a landscape full of hidden meaning. Another grand option is Plas Newydd on Anglesey, which provides stately surroundings against a backdrop of the Menai Strait and Snowdonia, ornate terrace gardens and a tree house to explore.

Other fabulous landscapes include Croome in Worcestershire – Capability Brown's first landscape garden, with lakes and rivers, bridges and follies, classical temples and walking trails. Clumber Park in Nottinghamshire is a spacious park perfect for cycling, orienteering or a gentle stroll followed by a picnic by the lake. Dinefwr Park in Carmarthenshire is another place to watch deer, in this case, a fallow herd that has been roaming the land here for a thousand years. Or take your own cricket tea to Sheffield Park in Sussex and watch a match on the historic pitch.

Florence Court in County Fermanagh is another property that has a beautiful park and gardens, and the surrounding forest offers miles of glorious walks and cycle trails in mountain scenery. For a different landscape altogether, try Blickling Estate in Norfolk, which features one of England's great Jacobean houses, formerly home to Henry VIII's second wife, Anne Boleyn, where parkland offers plenty of picnicking spots, a secret garden, ancient temple and an orangery.

Many properties have walled gardens or formal gardens, such as Beningbrough in North Yorkshire or at Eyam Hall in Derbyshire where you can enjoy pretty apple blossom or the roses in bloom, according to the season. Rose lovers might also like to spend time amid a national collection of old-fashioned roses held at Mottisfont in Hampshire. Hare Hill Garden in Cheshire also has a delightful walled garden with a giant wooden-hare trail through the trees for children and a hide for bird watching. At Wallington in Northumberland a woodland valley houses an enchanting walled garden with ponds, a nuttery, Edwardian conservatory and the intriguingly named Owl House. On a less formal note, try Lanhydrock in Cornwall for spectacular spring displays of magnolias, camellias and rhododendrons, or the magical gardens of Godolphin House, also in Cornwall, which have a feeling of being outside time.

Lovers of wild scenery might prefer Aira Force in Cumbria ('force' is a local word for a waterfall); here you'll also find woodland with red squirrels and a stunning view of Ullswater. In Wales, Aberdulais Falls, at Neath, near Port Talbot, allow a different exploration, of industrial archaeology and waterpower, whereas Lydford Gorge in Devon has orchard and woodland, home to numerous bird species, as well as the White Lady waterfall and the bubbling Devil's Cauldron. There are short scrambles for children of all ages and many hidden nooks in the curious shapes of Brimham Rocks in North Yorkshire.

More level and tranquil scenery can be found at Flatford Mill, Suffolk. This is great walking countryside, so absorb the atmosphere in the places that Constable knew and painted, or hire a boat and row down the river. Afterwards, visit a permanent Constable exhibition in a beautiful 16th-century thatched cottage. The Argory in County Armagh, too, offers tranquillity, where the mist rolls down to the River Blackwater and time stands still.

Coastal sites in the care of the Trust offer exceptional possibilities for picnic sites. Who could resist the opportunity to walk a little of the Cornish coastal path or to eat a picnic high above the churning waves or the Dorset coast with its fossil-hunting opportunities? Studland Beach in Dorset has shallow bathing water that is perfect for little children – take buckets and spades as well as a picnic. You can also visit the nearby ruins of Corfe Castle and relive childhood memories by seeing the inspiration behind Enid Blyton's Kirrin Castle in the *Famous Five*.

The Pembrokeshire coast in Wales has the delightfully named Barafundle, a jewel of a beach set between limestone cliffs and backed by dunes and woods for a real sand-in-your-sandwiches experience. Formby in Liverpool has miles of glorious sand, perfect for family outings, dog walking and watching wading birds on the shoreline. Connoisseurs of more offbeat locations might enjoy a stroll on the coast at Souter Lighthouse in Tyne and Wear, or at the other end of the country you can borrow picnic blankets from Mrs Knott's tea-room at South Foreland lighthouse, Dover.

Watch out also for special organised and themed events, such as a teddy bears picnic, pirates picnics, Georgian picnics, plays, or jazz or classical music concerts, and midsummer-eve picnics, or maybe something like a Bilberry Pick-nic amid the rugged landscape of the Marsden Moor Estate.

Containers and temperatures

Eating outside is the objective of a picnic, so carrying food is a priority. A walker out for a long day on the fells will want their vittles to be packed in lightweight wrappings that take up little space once the contents have been eaten, whereas a Glyndebourne-style picnic might demand most of the contents of the sideboard, plus numerous other accessories.

Think about cool-bags and ice packs for hot days, and flasks for keeping food or drink hot or cold (make sure you pre-heat flasks with boiling water or pre-chill them with ice, as appropriate). Flasks are good for soups and for carrying ice cubes or cold milk. It was quite normal for picnickers in the 19th century to take a kettle, a supply of tea, milk and sugar and a teapot along with them on any excursion (although Queen Victoria, rambling around the Scottish Highlands, seems to have been adept at sending her servants to the nearest cottage for boiling water). I have sympathy with the make-tea-on-the-spot theory. Hours in a flask doesn't do much for either tea or coffee, although I can appreciate the comfort of a hot drink immediately available on chilly, damp country walks. Carry milk separately for a better-tasting hot drink. For something more leisured and less weight-sensitive, though, a little camping stove and a kettle (I'm especially taken by the ones with silicone uppers in bright colours) is a good solution. Don't forget extra water as well as the tea, teapot (or teabags) and milk. A camping stove, of course, opens a world of possibilities in terms of cooked or reheated foods.

Picnic baskets come in many shapes and sizes, from the suitcase-like hamper with place settings for several people strapped into the lid, to the double-lidded shopping-basket type. The former have the blessing of tradition and neatness, but they are hopeless for carrying any food except wrapped sandwiches or cake because of the change in orientation if one wants to carry them by the handle. The shopping-basket type with a lid is better for delicate items and things that need to be kept upright, but for food ready set out on dishes or plates, a shallow open basket may be a better option. Put a frozen ice pack or two underneath anything that needs to be kept cold.

For the more practical option, picnic backpacks do a similar job in a form that is more convenient to carry. Less traditional, but with compartments for keeping food or drinks hot or cold, they could be the solution for those who want a more elaborate meal as part of a long walk or a hill climb.

When presenting food, consider the occasion. Lidded plastic boxes undoubtedly have their place, but they are utilitarian. Is your picnic supposed to be romantic, a reference to those elaborate 19th-century affairs, or a throwback to the glamorous 1930s? Or is it something that picks up on the current vogue for mid-20th-century design with 21st-century touches? I am not suggesting that the whole thing should be arranged like a photoshoot for a lifestyle magazine, but picnics are, at heart, frivolities and it's fun to look beyond the simply practical.

Mrs Beeton suggested large, well-corked jars for carrying semi-liquid mixtures such as stewed fruit: try a large preserving jar for carrying fruit salad, or smaller ones for dips, if weight isn't a problem. Ambrose Heath considered that sandwiches should be wrapped in waxed paper, each type in its own packet, with a slip of paper under the string telling what filling the enclosed contained. Clingfilm, not something envisaged by early-20th-century writers of science fiction, was far in the future at the time he was writing and, despite its utility, one might wish it still were. A waxed paper – or these days, silicone-coated baking parchment – packet, neatly tied with string or tape, is far more elegant; or see page 15 for how to keep sandwiches fresh for outdoor afternoon tea. Foil is also invaluable for wrapping all kinds of food, especially sandwiches and cold meat.

Serving bowls, plates and glasses are another matter. Good china and glassware is heavy and fragile, and should be reserved for only the most special of occasions. Mrs Leyel's solution was to buy cardboard plates and waxed paper linings to fit them, to be changed with each course so that one plate per person did duty all the way through the meal. I dislike card, or paper, plates on their own, but maybe what we think of as paper plates are actually what she considered as paper liners, and could be used as such with individual ceramic plates or brightly coloured plastic ones, one per guest. Coated paper tubs somehow don't share the disadvantages of paper plates and have a certain retro appeal. Another possibility is lightweight three-ply plates made of bamboo, now available via the Internet.

Lacquered bamboo is the environmentally friendly alternative, at least as serving bowls and trays. Leave anything cooked in a tin or mould in the container for carriage, and take a couple of serving spoons. Alternatively, look out for lightweight melamine or acrylic picnic ware, of which a wider selection appears every year. This is particularly good for bowls and drinking glasses. My one gripe with the latter is that they never seem to stack (and don't go for ones with stems – they are far too unstable). Paper cups are good for cold drinks, and you could try enamel mugs for hot soup.

Food for walks needs to be easily transportable with minimal packaging. The exception to this is a flask (or two) for keeping drinks hot or cold and for carrying soup. Even in the summer one can arrive at the top of a Welsh or Lake District mountain and discover the weather is significantly cooler or windier than expected, and soup is a welcome reviver; in any other season it is more than welcome.

Plastic wrappings always make me feel guilty because, despite their usefulness, they are an environmental curse. The zip-type plastic bag, however, is an amazingly useful item when carrying food, especially on walks or camping trips, when space and weight really count. They keep sandwiches fresh and can be used to carry meat in marinades for cooking on barbecues. They are also invaluable for dry flour mixtures for pancakes, and the like, for campfire cooking. Make up the mix simply by adding the right quantity of water to the mixture in the bag and squidging it together well with your hands, then pour the appropriate quantity straight from the bag onto a hot surface to cook.

Don't mention the spork!

The traditional fully fitted picnic hamper, whatever its drawbacks, solves the problem of carrying knives, forks and spoons. Much picnic food, especially sandwiches and things enclosed in pastry, don't need anything except fingers to help eat them, but bigger and more elegant meals do. Sporks – spoon–fork hybrids – belong, as far as I'm concerned, to the mix-with-water-and-then-heat category of packaged mountaineering food, but they are a solution for minimalists. Keep a collection of inexpensive lightweight cutlery for picnics (bright plastic handles mean you can see them in the grass when clearing up), or use disposable, biodegradable bamboo.

Take a small board and a sharp knife or two for cutting bread, cheese, fresh fruit and cake, a butter knife, and spoons for serving anything that needs them. Corkscrews are less essential in these days of screw-cap wine bottles, but it's always better to have one, and a bottle opener, in the pack. Add salt and pepper mills, bottled sauces or mustard as family tastes dictate, and other seasoning mixtures if desired. A tablecloth provides the arena for serving food, and differentiates it from running-around-playing-tag space. Cloth napkins are an excellent idea, and for any excursion involving food, whether it is to be cooked at the destination or merely consumed, a supply of paper napkins, wet wipes and kitchen paper is invaluable, as are a bag or two for collecting rubbish.

Comfort is important. It is unlikely, these days, that the chauffeur will remove the seats from the car so that the party can sit in them to admire the view, as Ambrose Heath recounted, but he is correct that comfort matters on a picnic. Take a couple of picnic rugs with waterproof backings to sit on, and a couple more without to wrap around yourself if the weather turns cold. Folding camping chairs are a good idea – more comfortable than the average rock, much drier than wet grass and a friendlier height for those who no longer have spring in their knees. A few cushions soften the ground for those who prefer to lounge.

Insects are always a potential hazard. Citronella tealights in holders, or flares, if they can be placed safely, are a possible solution against insects in the evening. Try to avoid ants' nests, accept that wasps will be a problem in late summer, and take insect repellent. For the latter, after years of exhaustive testing, I can only say that all seem to be equally inadequate against mosquitoes, although Avon's Skin So Soft moisturiser may just possibly work. The best solution is to find a spot with a slight breeze, which helps to keep biting insects at bay. If you do get bitten, a little bite-zapper device called Click Don't Scratch is quite effective in reducing the irritation.

Don't forget hats, cover-ups and sunscreen as well – you never know, they may be needed. Finally, always, always, take your rubbish home or dispose of it responsibly in designated bins.

Keeping sandwiches fresh

It is often a problem to keep sandwiches fresh when they need to be cut in advance, but here are some suggestions:

Clingfilm came to the rescue of the 'curly sandwich', a cliché of parties and picnics in the mid-20th century. It is neither elegant nor environmentally friendly, although indisputedly lightweight and easy to carry. One idea I've seen is to hollow out a very large, flattish round loaf by cutting a thin slice off the top to make a lid, and then carefully remove the crumb. This is used to make small sandwiches, which are then packed back into the cavity of the loaf; the 'lid' is replaced, and the outside of the loaf becomes the container. This is both an excellent way of keeping the contents fresh and a brilliant visual presentation. At the back of my mind, I can also hear the ghosts of my mother's and grandmother's generation murmuring about waste, although if picnicking by a river, the ducks would no doubt appreciate the remains.

My older female relatives would have used clean damp tea towels or napkins to cover sandwiches, removing them as the guests arrived. An even older alternative to this, now almost forgotten, was to cover the food with fresh green leaves. Cabbage leaves were one sort mentioned; fig or vine leaves look (and smell) prettier, if they are available.

One item that makes an effective container for tiny afternoon tea sandwiches and also looks pretty is a large and very fresh lettuce. Choose one with lots of outer leaves, and carefully trim the stem so that it stands level. Remove any unsightly and tattered parts, then carefully cut out the lettuce heart to leave a generous cup of the nicest, greenest outer leaves. Wash thoroughly, drain well, and keep covered in a cool place until needed.

Fill the hollow with sandwiches and pull the leaves over to enclose them until ready to eat. Store in a cool place (such as in a bowl in the fridge or a cool box), and it will keep the contents fresh for several hours. Iceberg lettuce is a good variety to use, but not the ones usually sold in supermarkets that have been reduced to the inner leaves only. If nothing better is available, a large cos lettuce can be cut in half lengthways and the heart removed from each half to give a long, narrow two-part container.

How to use this book

The recipes in this book are grouped loosely into menus with specific occasions or groups in mind. Starting with a simple afternoon tea and other recipes requiring the back-up of a kitchen, they move further away into open-air cooking, sometimes with an absolute minimum of equipment. Although I've organised the recipes in ways that seem to me to work especially well together, there is no intention of suggesting limits to any single idea or event, so use them in any combination as you prefer.

AN AFTERNOON TEA PICNIC

This menu is based on the quintessential English afternoon-tea idea: not too challenging in terms of venue and relying on small and dainty food. I think of it as a small treat for those who have some reason for staying close to home – for entertaining an elderly relative with limited mobility, someone who is recovering from an illness, a new mother who'd rather not venture too far with her infant. The recipes could be scaled up for a small family celebration such as a christening, and there is no reason why the food shouldn't be packed in a basket and taken further afield.

Presentation is important: look out for a pretty tablecloth and china to lay a table with a cloth and a posy of flowers in a sheltered spot outdoors. The food is mostly finger food; tea knives will be needed for the scones, and cake forks for the chocolate cake, which has a sticky icing. The meal should, of course, be served with tea to drink, freshly made in a nice teapot.

Other possible recipes or sandwich fillings for this event include: Bridge Rolls and Egg Mayonnaise (pages 32–33), Oriental Filling (page 85), Asparagus Filling (page 86) and Banana and Stem Ginger Cake (page 36). For a special occasion, add a favourite celebration cake.

Mrs Maher's Perfect Cucumber Sandwiches

Makes about 20 very small sandwiches

1 cucumber, peeled

1 scant teaspoon salt

1 teaspoon tarragon vinegar (optional)

10 very thin slices (less than 5mm thick) from 1 small, good-quality white loaf, 1 day old

softened butter, for spreading

lettuce container, to serve (optional) (see page 15)

Tiny cucumber sandwiches are a classic for summer afternoon teas in England, but like all simple things they need attention to detail if they are to be made well. A friend describing how her mother made these for bridge parties provided the perfect method. They can be made 2–3 hours in advance, or longer if kept fresh as described on page 15.

Using a knife, cut the cucumber into the thinnest slices possible (only use a food processor or mandoline if you are confident of making very thin slices, not thickish or uneven ones). Put the slices in a colander and lightly sprinkle with salt. Leave for 1 hour to drain.

Drain as much of the liquid as possible and pat the slices dry using kitchen paper or a clean tea towel. Season the cucumber with the vinegar, if using.

Spread the bread slices thinly on one side with butter, making sure you spread it close to the edges.

Distribute the cucumber over 5 of the buttered slices. Don't overlap too much. Top with the remaining bread. Press each sandwich down with the palm of your hand, then take a rolling pin and roll across each one gently but firmly a few times so that the sandwich sticks together well.

Trim off the crusts to make each sandwich as close to a square as possible, then cut each one diagonally to give 4 little triangular pieces. Arrange on a pretty dish or use a lettuce container. Cover and chill until needed.

Poached Salmon Mayonnaise

Makes 20 very small sandwiches

200g poached salmon, skinned and boned

2 tablespoons mayonnaise

the feathery leaves from a sprig of dill, finely chopped

Ravigote Butter (see below) or ordinary butter

10 very thin slices of white bread

salt

These sandwiches have a pretty contrast of green and pink in the middle and are an unusual shape that is derived from the sandwiches made in Harry's Bar in Venice. The recipe uses Ravigote Butter but can be replaced with ordinary butter if you prefer, or with Watercress Butter (see page 59). Ravigote Butter contains salad burnet, which is easily grown or can be foraged in traditionally managed meadows in the late spring and early summer. It can be recognised by its small oval leaves, which have serrated edges. If you can't find it, omit it, and increase the quantities of other herbs or substitute parsley instead.

Flake the salmon using a fork and mix with the mayonnaise and dill, adding a little salt to taste if necessary.

Spread the Ravigote Butter over each bread slice, making sure you spread it close to the edges.

Put a quarter of the filling down the centre of a slice in a bolster-like roll, running from the top to the bottom crust. Top with another slice of bread, so that it curves over the filling, and press the long sides of the slices together well.

Trim the top and bottom so that the filling is exposed at the ends, then cut off the crusts from the sides. Slice across the sandwich at about 1cm intervals so that you have 4 little domed sandwiches, each with a circle of filling in the middle of 2 strips of bread. Repeat using the remaining bread and filling. Cover and chill until needed.

Ravigote Butter

Makes about 370g

30g fresh chervil leaves

30g fresh tarragon leaves

30g fresh chives leaves

30g fresh salad burnet leaves (optional)

250g salted butter

This recipe makes quite a large quantity, but it freezes well. Divide the butter into suitable portions before freezing. It is good with any kind of fish, with chicken, pork or vegetables.

Put the herbs in a bowl and pour over enough boiling water to cover. Drain immediately and refresh in cold water. Squeeze dry in kitchen paper.

Put them into a blender or food processor and whizz to chop them, then add the butter and process again to make a paste.

Sweet Parmesan and Lemon Scones

150g self-raising flour, plus extra for dusting

60g butter, cut into small pieces

60g caster sugar

40g good-quality Parmesan cheese, freshly grated (don't be tempted to use ready grated)

finely grated zest of ½ lemon

80ml buttermilk, or as needed

1 medium egg, beaten

whipped or clotted cream, and lemon curd, to serve

Using strong, salty Parmesan in sweet recipes seems outlandish to us, but the cheese has deep, complex flavours, including floral and nutty notes, which are surprisingly good with sweetness. Make this mixture into small scones, which are best eaten on the day they are made, just cooled.

Preheat the oven to 200°C and dust a baking sheet with flour. Using your fingertips, rub the butter into the flour until it resembles fine crumbs.

Stir in the sugar, Parmesan and lemon zest. Gradually add the buttermilk and bring the mixture together with your fingertips to make a soft, slightly sticky dough.

Turn onto a floured work surface and knead just enough to bring the mixture into a coherent mass. Quickly roll out to about 2cm thick and cut into circles using a 5cm biscuit cutter (dip the cutter in flour after each use if the mixture seems sticky). Gather the scraps together and re-roll to cut as many scones as possible.

Put the dough on the floured baking tray and brush with beaten egg. Bake for 10–15 minutes until risen and golden. Cool on a wire rack. Serve with cream and lemon curd.

Queen of Sheba Cake

Makes 8 small slices

120g unsalted butter, plus extra for greasing

120g dark chocolate, 60% cocoa solids

2 large eggs, separated, plus 1 large egg yolk

120g caster sugar

60g plain flour, sifted

For the icing

100g granulated sugar

50g unsalted butter

50ml milk

50g dark chocolate, 60% cocoa solids

Our ancestors might have considered this a trifle decadent for afternoon tea, but it is very good. The portions are small, but then afternoon tea is supposed to be dainty. I think it's perfect on its own, but add a little crème fraîche and a few raspberries on the side if you like.

Preheat the oven to 200°C, then grease and line a 20 x 20 x 2cm square tin with baking parchment. Melt the butter and chocolate in a heatproof bowl over a saucepan of gently simmering water, making sure the base of the bowl doesn't touch the water.

Put the egg yolks and sugar in a mixing bowl and stir with a wooden spoon until amalgamated, then beat well using an electric mixer. Still beating, trickle in the chocolate and butter mixture and mix well to combine. Fold in the flour.

Put the egg whites into a clean, dry, grease-free bowl and whisk until they form soft peaks. Fold the whites into the mixture. Quickly pour the batter into the prepared tin, give it a light shake to make sure it is level, and bake for 20 minutes – keep an eye on it after 15 minutes, and turn the heat down if the cake shows signs of overcooking. It is done when a skewer inserted into the centre of the mixture comes out clean. Remove from the oven and leave in the tin. While the cake is still warm make the icing.

Put all the icing ingredients in a saucepan over a medium-low heat and heat gently, stirring, until the butter and chocolate have melted and sugar dissolved. Bring to the boil, then reduce the heat and simmer very gently for 5 minutes. At this point, test as you would jam, by dropping a little mixture on a cold saucer and putting it in the fridge for a moment. It should form a skin that wrinkles when pushed with a finger. Cook for 1–2 minutes more if it seems on the thin side.

Pour the icing over the warm cake. Leave the cake and icing strictly alone for 12–24 hours.

Remove the cake from the tin, and carefully peel off the paper, then put the cake on a suitable serving dish. Cut into four squares, then cut each square diagonally to give eight triangles.

If you prefer a larger cake, make two of the size given, then ice one for the top and sandwich them together with a little apricot preserve in between.

CHILDREN'S PICNIC IN THE PARK

———

This chapter features easy, child-friendly dips and nibbles for a midday feast between building dens and catching minnows. The menu is finger food, which needs a few serving dishes and bowls, but otherwise a minimum of plates and cutlery. There's a case to be made for paper plates and cups, as light to carry and easily disposable, but if the budget runs to something more, there is plenty of well-designed acrylic picnic ware available. Choose plates with bright colours and attractive patterns, as youngsters eat with their eyes as much as anyone else, probably more so. Set the food out nicely and use brightly coloured cloths and napkins.

Although it's best to carry the dips, the crudités and filled rolls in a cool-bag, the rest can be packed into cake tins or nice boxes. Wet wipes are essential, and take along bottled water and other drinks as appropriate. What else? A picnic rug or two, perhaps some cushions, sunscreen for if the weather is kind, and sweaters and wraps for if it isn't.

Take also:

- Fruit in season – small children might prefer it made into 'kebabs' of raw fruit – orange sections, pieces of peach, melon, kiwi fruit or pineapple, strawberries, and other fruit in season, threaded onto wooden skewers.
- Tea, coffee or other drinks for the grown-ups.
- Soft drinks or fruit juice for the children as an alternative to lemonade.
- Crisps or other savoury nacks as desired.

Dips and Things to Dip in Them

You can buy dips, of course, or use bought ones as a base, tarted up with extra herbs, spices, a little olive oil or a scattering of toasted pine nuts. Or you can make dips and sauces that aren't available from the shops, such as the two given here. Both can be made the day before, and both are good as side dishes for barbecued fish or chicken, should the mood lean towards something more substantial. (See also Baba Ganoush, page 122, Tapenade, page 102, and Avocado Salsa, page 144.)

Green Goddess Dip

Makes about 350g

1 large avocado

100ml buttermilk

2 teaspoons finely chopped fresh chives

2 teaspoons finely chopped fresh tarragon

2 teaspoons finely chopped fresh flat leaf parsley

2 teaspoons finely chopped fresh basil

juice of ½ lemon

1 small garlic clove, roughly chopped

½ teaspoon Dijon mustard

½ teaspoon finely grated lemon zest

1 tablespoon white wine vinegar

a pinch of chilli powder

½ teaspoon salt

2 anchovy fillets or ½ teaspoon ground cumin

A recipe from the west coast of the USA, this dip has many variations: some use mayonnaise or soured cream, some omit the avocado and some add watercress or a little mint. The parsley, tarragon, basil and chives, garlic or shallot seem to be fairly constant.

Put all the ingredients in a blender or food processor and blend well.

Scrape out into a pretty serving bowl and chill until needed.

Skordalia (Greek Garlic Sauce)

Makes about 450g

125g crustless stale white bread
4–5 garlic cloves, to taste
50g blanched almonds
180ml olive oil
2–4 teaspoons red wine vinegar, to taste
salt

Skordalia is a dip based on either bread or potato and strongly flavoured with garlic. The character of the sauce depends a lot on the olive oil: extra virgin gives a strong, peppery olive flavour; use a lighter one, or a mixture of the two, for a milder version. The almonds are not essential but add interest to the texture.

Put the bread in a bowl and cover with water, then leave to soak for a few minutes. Remove the bread and squeeze well to remove as much water as possible.

Put the garlic, ½ teaspoon salt and the almonds in a blender or food processor and process for a few seconds to make a rough paste. Add the bread and pulse to make a paste.

With the motor running, gradually pour in the oil to make a smooth mixture. Taste, and adjust the seasoning using the vinegar, plus a little more salt if needed.

For a potato version, substitute 300g freshly cooked mashed potato for the soaked bread, and make the dip by processing the garlic, salt, almonds and a third of the oil together. Stir the mixture into the potato, then add the remaining oil little by little.

Things to Dip

To serve, put your chosen dips in nice bowls (lightweight plastic picnic ware is appropriate here) and surround with a choice of items for dipping. Try an array of vegetable crudités — little oval tomatoes, halved lengthways, slender white and pink 'French Breakfast' radishes, small wedges of fennel bulb, cucumber, carrot or red pepper cut into sticks are classic choices. Or add new-season young carrots boiled for 2 minutes and baby new potatoes boiled until tender and halved lengthways.

Bread sticks, bought or home-made, add a change of texture and crunch, as do Savoury Palmiers (below). If you want to avoid commercially made savoury snacks but would still like something salty with lots of flavour, try Paprika Cheese Biscuits (page 64), baked as straws instead of cut into round biscuits. Children of any age also appreciate good sausages, nicely cooked and well drained, and allowed to go cold.

Savoury Palmiers

Makes 18–20

flour, for dusting

250g puff pastry, home-made or purchased, and thawed if frozen

50g Pesto Genovese, home-made (see page 89) or purchased

These are easy to make, especially if you buy ready-made pastry, and are good with dips or as a nibble with drinks. They are best on the day they are made but will keep for a few days in an airtight tin. Tapenade (page 102), Garlic Butter (page 196) or Ravigote Butter (page 20) are good alternatives instead of the pesto.

Preheat the oven to 220°C. Dust a work surface with flour and roll the pastry into a narrow rectangle about 12 x 40cm.

Trim the edges with a sharp knife to make them straight. Spread the pesto lengthways down the centre in a strip about 6cm wide. Take it right to the edges at the short ends.

Fold in the long edges so that they meet in the centre, covering the filling. Then fold lengthways again. Use a sharp knife to cut the pastry into slices at 2cm intervals.

Put cut-side down and well spaced apart on two baking trays and bake for 12–15 minutes, until the pastry is nicely expanded and golden. Cool on a wire rack.

Sausage Rolls

Makes 20 small sausage rolls or
8 large ones

600g good-quality sausage meat (buy
your favourite sausages and remove the
skins)

extra seasoning, to taste, such as 1
teaspoon finely chopped fresh sage
leaves and 2 teaspoons finely chopped
fresh thyme leaves

flour, for dusting
250g puff pastry, thawed if frozen
1 medium egg, beaten

I've yet to meet a child who doesn't like sausage rolls, and most adults seem to like them too. They are very simple to make and home-made ones are generally much nicer than bought.

Preheat the oven to 200°C. Put the sausage meat in a bowl and stir it to make a homogenous mass, adding the extra seasoning if needed.

Dust a work surface with flour and roll out the pastry to a rectangle roughly 32 x 15cm. Cut in half lengthways.

Divide the sausage meat into 2 and form into long rolls the length of the pastry. Put the meat along the long edge of each piece of pastry. Brush water down one side and roll up neatly, then cut each in 10 short lengths (for little rolls) or 4 (for large ones).

Transfer to a baking tray and brush with the beaten egg. Bake small rolls for 20–25 minutes or large ones for 25–30 minutes until puffed and golden. Cool on a wire rack.

Bridge Rolls

Makes 16 small rolls

1 teaspoon dried yeast

a pinch of sugar

200–250ml hand-hot water

450g strong plain bread flour, plus extra for dusting

1 teaspoon salt

30g lard, cut into small pieces

2 medium eggs

1 medium egg, beaten, or milk or cream, to glaze

Bridge rolls were a treat at picnics, tea parties and cold suppers in my childhood, usually filled with a mixture of mashed hard-boiled egg and salad cream. Whatever is put in them, they should be tiny – a couple of mouthfuls – and I find the only way to get this size is to make them myself. The dough also makes good burger buns (see page 155).

Put the yeast, sugar and half the water in a jug and leave in a warm place for a few minutes until it begins to froth.

Put the flour in a large bowl and sprinkle in the salt. Rub in the lard. Add the yeast mixture, the 2 eggs and about half the remaining water. Mix to make a soft, slightly sticky dough. If it seems a little dry, add some more water, then knead until the dough becomes a smooth, coherent mass. Cover the bowl with clingfilm and leave in a warm place for 1 hour or until the dough has doubled in size.

Preheat the oven to 200°C and grease a baking tray. Knock back the dough and divide it into 16 pieces. Dust your hands and the work surface with flour. Shape each piece of dough into a 4cm long roll.

Space the rolls equally on the tray and brush with egg, milk or cream. Leave to rise for 30 minutes–1 hour until they have doubled in size. Bake for 10 minutes, until golden.

Cool the rolls wrapped in a clean tea towel to help keep the crust soft and tender.

Egg Mayonnaise

Makes enough to fill 10 bridge rolls, or 20 tiny afternoon tea sandwiches or 4 large rolls

This filling is simplicity itself, and an old favourite. It can also be used in afternoon tea sandwiches (especially the Harry's Bar type, see Poached Salmon Mayonnaise, page 20), or in large soft bread rolls as part of a walker's pack.

4 hard-boiled medium eggs, peeled and chopped

6 tablespoons mayonnaise

a bunch of watercress, coarse stalks removed

salt and ground black pepper

Mix the eggs with the mayonnaise and add a little salt and a generous amount of pepper.

Chop about half the watercress (if it is a bit spindly you may need a more) and stir it into the mixture. Fill the sandwiches and use the extra cress to garnish them.

Cream Cheese and Ginger Sandwich Filling

Makes enough to fill 10 bridge rolls or 20 very small sandwiches

The idea for this slightly sweet filling for sandwiches was among those listed by Ambrose Heath in Good Sandwiches and Picnic Dishes *(1947). Oriental Filling (page 85) is another cream cheese filling, given an interesting texture with the addition of nuts.*

60g preserved stem ginger in syrup, or to taste, drained

250g full-fat soft cheese

10 very thin slices (less than 5mm thick) from 1 small wholemeal loaf, 1 day old

softened butter, for spreading

Chop the stem ginger into tiny cubes a little less than 5mm along each side. They should be large enough to be visible, but not so large that they make a very lumpy filling.

Beat the soft cheese smooth, then stir in the chopped ginger and mix well.

Spread the bread slices thinly on one side with the butter, making sure you spread it close to the edges.

Spread the cream cheese mixture evenly over 5 of the buttered slices and top with the remaining bread, then press each one down gently. Trim off the crusts to make each sandwich as close to a square as possible, then cut each sandwich again to give 4 tiny square sandwiches.

Nutella, Raspberry and Chocolate Chip Muffins

Makes 24 mini muffins or about 8
regular muffins

200g Nutella
2 medium eggs
100g self-raising flour
80g dark chocolate chips
80g frozen raspberries
1–2 tablespoons milk

This recipe is specifically intended for mini-muffins, something small children seem to appreciate, but the mixture can be made into regular-size muffins if you prefer. They can, of course, be used for any picnic as preferred. Children might enjoy helping to make these as well.

Preheat the oven to 200°C and line 24 mini muffin pans or 8 regular muffin pans with paper cases. Put the Nutella in a bowl (it is helpful to use one with a pouring spout) and break the eggs into it. Stir well until it is amalgamated into a smooth mixture.

Stir in the flour, followed by the chocolate chips and frozen raspberries (break any large ones up). The mixture should be quite runny; add the milk to slacken it if it seems on the stiff side.

Quickly divide the batter among the muffin cases. Bake for 15–20 minutes, testing after 15 with a cocktail stick: if it comes out clean, they are done.

Cool on a wire rack.

Banana and Stem Ginger Cake

100g butter, softened, plus extra for greasing

100g soft light brown sugar

2 medium eggs

1 tablespoon golden syrup, or syrup from the preserved stem ginger jar

2 medium very ripe bananas, mashed

150g self-raising flour

1 teaspoon baking powder

½ teaspoon mixed spice

50–60g preserved stem ginger in syrup, to taste, drained and chopped into small cubes

50–60g walnuts (optional), to taste, roughly chopped

Here is a lighter, spiced version of banana cake. The walnuts add a pleasant crunchy contrast in texture but can be left out if you prefer. It can be made a couple of days ahead.

Preheat the oven to 180°C and grease and line a 20 x 20 x 2cm square tin with non-stick baking parchment.

Quick method
Put all the ingredients except the stem ginger and walnuts, if using, into a deep mixing bowl and blend with a stick blender for 1–2 minutes, just until everything is mixed (don't worry if there are a few small lumps). Stir in the ginger and walnuts.

Alternative conventional creaming method
Beat the butter and brown sugar together until the mixture is light and pale. Beat in the eggs, one after another. Stir in the syrup and bananas. Don't worry if the mixture curdles a little at this point.

Sift in the flour, baking powder and spice, and stir to combine, then stir in the stem ginger and walnuts, if using.

Put the mixture in the prepared tin and bake for 30–35 minutes, or until a skewer comes out clean when pushed into the centre of the mixture.

Cool in the tin and cut into 4 along the top and sides to give 16 pieces, or cut into 2 along the top and 4 along the sides for 8 larger pieces.

Lemonade

Makes about 500ml

450g sugar
2 kaffir lime leaves (optional)
finely grated zest and juice of 1 lemon
10g citric acid (optional)
ice cubes, to serve

This recipe makes me nostalgic for the lemon cordials my mother made in summer. The citric acid, which can be purchased from pharmacies, adds flavour and helps the cordial to store well. The kaffir lime leaves are available frozen from Asian grocers. The packs are quite large but they keep well in the freezer, and one or two leaves can be taken out as necessary. For an alcoholic drink made with this cordial, see page 60.

Put the sugar and 350ml water in a saucepan over a medium-low heat and stir to dissolve. Add the lime leaves, and the lemon zest and juice, then bring to the boil. Turn off the heat.

Add the citric acid, if using. Allow the mixture to cool, then strain and transfer to a sterilised bottle. Dilute to taste and serve over ice.

THE BIG FAMILY
AND FRIENDS PICNIC

———

All generations of the family are looking forward to a midday feast in a beauty spot. But when catering for a large picnic like this there are many different tastes to be accommodated, as well as the usual uncertainty about the weather. The food is a main event. What should you take with you?

All families have their own favourites, whether it's cold cuts and salads or particular types of sandwiches. I'm not trying to cover all options but will suggest a few more unusual items that travel well. Make it a bring-a-dish occasion, where a number of people each contribute an item, to give a range of old and new ideas. Remember to pack essential equipment, such as rugs, cushions, chairs, cutlery, plates, paper napkins, wet wipes and bags for any rubbish you might have.

Other things that could be added are:

- A roast of beef. Allow it to cool, carve it into slices, then reassemble and wrap in foil. Take mustard or horseradish cream to serve with it.
- Cold cooked ham. Treat it in the same way as the beef, and remember to pack the mustard.
- Cold roast chicken, whole or in portions. This could be prepared with the barbecue rub (Seasoning Mix for Chicken) on page 144 but then roasted rather than barbecued.
- Cooked sausages. Drain the excess fat, then cool them before packing in foil or wrapping in greaseproof paper.

Whatever else you take, add:

- Good bread (and a small board and a knife for cutting it), plus butter.
- Some ready-mixed salads (see Coleslaw, page 157, Greek Cabbage Salad, page 125, Potato Salad, page 41, Sweet Pepper Relish, page 148, Avocado Salsa, page 144).
- Some salad leaves (people never eat as much green salad as you think they will) and a bottle of French dressing.
- A punnet of little tomatoes, to be eaten as finger food, or some crudités (see page 29), plus favourite dips to go with them.
- Salt, pepper, salad dressing or mayonnaise.

For a dessert on these occasions, cheese and fresh fruit is often more satisfactory than an elaborate cake or pudding. Try, according to the season:

- A piece of quality Wensleydale cheese with some fresh apricots or cherries.
- Perfectly ripe Brie with a beautiful bunch of grapes.
- Blue Stilton or Gorgonzola dolce and a bowl of fresh figs.
- A chunk of Montgomery's Cheddar with some English-grown pears or apples.
- Take extra bread, butter and biscuits to eat with it.
- You could follow Mrs Beeton's lead and take stewed fruit (gooseberries, apricots, plums, pears) in jars, with thick cream or yogurt to accompany it.

To drink:

- The Strawberry Cider (contains alcohol) on page 41. Take, according to taste and the age range, other cold soft or alcoholic drinks and ice to chill them, as well as bottled water.
- Tea was always considered essential at such events in the past, and picnickers – or possibly their servants – would light a campfire or use a portable patent stove such as a Primus to boil a kettle. Camping stoves make this easy, so take one of these, plus a supply of fuel and a kettle. (Today you can buy one of the brightly coloured metal and silicone kettles, which achieve combining good design and cheerful modernity while sturdily maintaining the English ideal of a cup of tea whatever the circumstances.)
- Pack a teapot and leaf tea, plus water, milk, a jug and sugar as needed. Also pack cups (with saucers, naturally – no need to let standards drop because you're outside).

Potato Salad

Serves 6–8

Dill and gherkins perk up the flavours in this old favourite.

750g small-medium new potatoes, scrubbed

1 teaspoon Dijon mustard

75g mayonnaise, home-made or good-quality purchased

150g whole milk natural yogurt

2 tablespoons finely chopped dill, plus a few sprigs to garnish

4–6 medium pickled gherkins, chopped into small dice

a few nicely shaped and coloured lettuce leaves

salt and ground black pepper

dill sprigs, to garnish

Boil the potatoes whole until just tender. Drain and, when cool enough to handle, remove the skins. Cut the flesh into cubes or crumble it into irregular pieces.

Put the mustard in a bowl. Add the mayonnaise, yogurt, dill and gherkins, then stir well. Taste, and add salt and pepper as desired. Mix again, then fold in the potatoes.

Line a serving bowl with lettuce leaves so that they project a little way above the rim. Spoon in the potato salad, and garnish the top with dill sprigs.

Strawberry Cider

Makes 1½ litres

Summery and delicious, this cider is perfect for warm afternoons sitting in dappled shade. Prepare the strawberry mixture for your picnic and transport it in a plastic box in a well-chilled cooler, with the cider in bottles and the ice in a flask. Decant the strawberry mix into a jug and add the chilled cider and ice at the destination.

500g strawberries, hulled

2 tablespoons caster sugar

juice of 1 orange

1 litre sweet cider, chilled

plenty of ice cubes

Crush the strawberries lightly using a fork or a potato masher. Put in a large bowl or jug. Scatter over the sugar and add the orange juice. Leave to macerate for 1 hour, then add the cider. Serve over plenty of ice.

Chilled Cucumber Cream

Serves 8–10 (120ml servings)

200ml double cream

300ml buttermilk

2 large cucumbers, peeled

2 garlic cloves, crushed

2 tablespoons olive oil

1 tablespoon fresh dill leaves, finely chopped, plus dill sprigs, to garnish

salt

Cooling and delicious, this creamy soup is perfect for a warm day. Serve in small glasses garnished with dill sprigs.

Heat the cream in a small saucepan over a medium heat until it boils. Put the buttermilk in a bowl and stir in the cream, then leave to cool.

Cut the cucumbers lengthways into quarters and remove the seeds. Dice the flesh into tiny cubes and put them in a bowl. Mix with the garlic and oil. Stir in the cooled cream mixture, with the chopped dill and 1 teaspoon salt. Leave for 3 hours or overnight if possible, to allow the flavours to blend.

Stir in 200ml water, or a little more if you prefer a thinner soup. If you like, blend half the soup until smooth for a less chunky texture. Taste and add more salt if needed. Serve in small glasses garnished with dill sprigs. Give each person a teaspoon to scoop out the cucumber pieces at the end.

Rillettes

Makes about 450g

1 teaspoon black peppercorns
1 teaspoon coriander seeds
1.5 kg belly pork
200g pork flare fat or 100g goose fat
2 teaspoons salt
2 star anise
2 garlic cloves, cut into fine slivers
a good pinch of dried chilli flakes
100ml white wine or water

Rillettes are a kind of potted pork traditional to French cookery. They keep and transport well and make robust outdoor food. Eat them with good bread and the little pickled gherkins known to the French as cornichons. *Try to buy a fatty piece of pork, or ask the butcher if he has some pork flare fat that you can have to add to a lean piece. If this isn't possible, some goose fat can be added instead, but don't be tempted to use ordinary lard. Star anise is not the traditional spice but it gives a good flavour. The cooking time is long, but no attention should be required during this. It's ideal for the slow oven of an Aga.*

Preheat the oven to 130°C. Grind the peppercorns and coriander seeds in a grinder or mortar and pestle. Remove any bones from the pork by running a knife between them and the meat and removing them in one piece (they can be barbecued as pork ribs). Cut off the skin and fat, making sure that there is no meat attached to the fat. Cut the meat into slices roughly 1cm wide, then cut these across to make chunks 1 x 2cm.

Put the skin and fat in the base of a roasting tin or casserole, then the meat in one layer and add all the other ingredients. Cover with two layers of foil, sealing well, and the lid if the container has one. Put in the oven and cook undisturbed for 4 hours.

Remove from the oven and uncover. You should have very well-cooked, soft pieces of meat swimming in fat and liquid. Put a sieve over a heatproof bowl and pour everything through it. Allow the fat to drain thoroughly.

Put the meat on a large platter or in a shallow bowl. Pick out the skin and the star anise, and discard. Take 2 forks and use them to shred the meat, reducing it to a fibrous paste. When all is done, taste to check the seasoning – it should taste quite highly seasoned. Add more salt and pepper if needed.

Pack the meat into sterilised jars, pushing it down firmly. Spoon some of the fat over the top to form a layer and leave to cool. The rillettes will keep for a week or so in the fridge. To store for longer, transfer to the freezer. Use the jellied juices from under the fat to add to stir-fries or a pork casserole.

Spiced Salt or Dukkah

Makes about 50g

25g hazelnuts
15g sesame seeds
½ teaspoon black peppercorns
1 teaspoon cumin seeds
1 teaspoon dried thyme
1 teaspoon salt

Dukkah is an Egyptian seasoning mix, usually based on hazelnuts mixed with salt and various seeds and spices. It is very good with hard-boiled eggs, for dipping bread and raw vegetables and as a seasoning for plain grilled meat. It also keeps well in a cool, dark place.

Preheat the oven to 160°C. Put the hazelnuts on a baking tray and toast in the oven for 10–15 minutes until pale gold. Put the hazelnuts in a in a clean tea towel and rub off the skins. Toast the sesame seeds in the same way – they may take a little less time, so watch them carefully.

Put the peppercorns and cumin in a dry frying pan over a low heat and toast them until they give off an appetising aroma. Put the nuts, sesame seeds, spices and thyme in a spice grinder or use a mortar and pestle and grind to a coarse powder. Stir in the salt. Store in an airtight jar.

Chinese Marbled Tea Eggs

Makes 8

8 medium eggs

1 star anise

2 tablespoons soy sauce

2 tablespoons tea leaves (orange pekoe
or Assam)

*Hard-boiled eggs are a British picnic staple. If you are catering for a large number
of people and want to splash out, acquire eggs of different colours and sizes – deep
brown, perfectly white, pale blue – from different breeds of hen, plus smaller
bantam eggs and tiny quail eggs, and serve on an attractive plate or in a basket for
everyone to peel their own. Alternatively, use ordinary eggs to make these prettily
patterned long-cooked eggs. Use the freshest ones you can buy.*

Cover the eggs with water and bring to the boil, then boil gently for 8
minutes. Drain and run cold water over them until just cool enough to
handle.

Gently tap all over each shell with the back of a teaspoon to create a network
of fine cracks. Return the eggs to the pan, add all the other ingredients and
enough water to cover. Bring to the boil, then simmer gently for another
30 minutes.

Remove from the heat and leave for at least 8 hours or overnight. Peel the
eggs to reveal the marbled pattern. To make them easier to peel, about 30
minutes beforehand, discard the mixture they were cooked in. Roll the
eggs on a board or hard work surface so the shells crack more. Put them
in a pan of fresh cold water for 15–20 minutes, and the shells should be
easier to remove.

Brendon's Bacon and Egg Pie

Serves 6–8

150g unsmoked back bacon rashers

2 tablespoons finely chopped flat leaf parsley leaves

8–10 medium eggs

1 medium egg, beaten, or milk or cream, to glaze

salt and ground black pepper

tomato ketchup, to serve

For the pastry
250g plain flour, plus extra for dusting
a pinch of salt
125g lard

Bacon and egg pie — something I thought was forgotten — is alive and well and a favourite picnic food in Australia. A friend from Melbourne supplied a few details that make it better than any versions I remember from school dinners. It's best made in an old-fashioned shallow pie dish or plate with sloping sides.

Preheat the oven to 220°C and put a baking tray inside to heat. To make the pastry, put the flour and salt in a large bowl and rub into the lard with your fingertips until it resembles fine crumbs. Using a fork, stir in 4–5 tablespoons cold water until the dough just begins to hold together. Bring the dough together into a ball and knead lightly for a few seconds. Wrap in clingfilm and chill for 30 minutes before using.

Cut the bacon into pieces roughly 2 x 1cm and cook gently in a frying pan over a medium heat without any additional fat until the lean is pink and the fat is white and opaque. Leave to cool.

Take two-thirds of the pastry and roll it out to make a circle 25cm in diameter. Use this to line a 20cm pie plate. Scatter the bacon pieces over the pastry and sprinkle with a little of the parsley. Season with black pepper.

Break the eggs one by one into a saucer (trying not to break the yolks) and gently slide each one onto the top of the bacon. Add salt, pepper and parsley to each as you go.

Roll out the remaining pastry to make a circle large enough to cover the top of the pie. Brush the edge of the pastry base in the pie dish with water and cover with the pastry lid, trimming nicely and crimping well together. Cut a hole in the middle and brush over with beaten egg.

Put the pie on the heated tray and cook for 15 minutes, then turn the heat down to 180°C and bake for a further 10 minutes to set the eggs. The pie is excellent hot, warm or cold. The traditional Australian accompaniment is tomato ketchup, which helps to cut the slightly dry richness of the yolks.

Georgian Herb and Egg Pie

Serves 6–8

60g long grain rice

4 medium eggs

2 tablespoons light olive oil or other oil

200g spring onions, chopped

50g fresh tarragon leaves, chopped

100g spinach or watercress leaves, chopped

1 teaspoon salt

flour, for dusting

500g puff pastry, thawed if frozen

1 teaspoon softened butter

ground black pepper

Transcaucasia has always been a region of good food. On holiday there, I was amazed by the abundance and importance of fresh herbs used in the local dishes, reflected in this unusual pie based on one from the Republic of Georgia. Tarragon, the principal flavouring, varies in strength and can be on the bitter side. Using other leaves helps to soften the effect while retaining a generally 'green' note.

Preheat the oven to 200°C. Cook the rice in plenty of boiling water until tender. Drain and leave to cool. Hard-boil 3 of the eggs and peel them.

Heat the oil in a saucepan over a medium-low heat and fry the spring onions, tarragon and spinach leaves gently for 3 minutes. Chop the hard-boiled eggs and stir them and the rice into the spinach mixture in the pan. Leave to cool.

Stir in the salt and plenty of pepper. Separate the fourth egg and stir in the white.

Dust a work surface with flour and roll out about two-thirds of the pastry to give a rectangle about 45 x 30cm. Neaten the edges. Spread the cooled herb and egg mixture over the middle of this, leaving about 4cm around the edges. Fold these up to make a frame around the filling, making sure the corners are neatly trimmed and carefully sealed.

Roll out the remaining pastry to give a rectangle large enough to cover the exposed filling and overlap the folded-up edges. Brush these with water, then cover and press gently to seal. Transfer the pie to a large baking sheet.

Beat the remaining egg yolk with the butter and use this mixture to brush over the top of the pie. Bake for 25–30 minutes, until the pastry is golden, well risen and cooked through. Leave to cool.

The pie is at its best eaten the same day, fairly soon after cooking while the pastry is still crisp, but it will still be good the following day.

Kuku-e-Sabzi or Persian Herb Omelette

Serves 6–8

50g fresh flat leaf parsley leaves

20g fresh coriander leaves

50g fresh dill leaves

50g fresh fenugreek leaves

50g leek

2 garlic cloves, crushed

1 teaspoon black peppercorns

½ teaspoon cumin seeds

seeds of 3–4 cardamom pods

a small piece of cinnamon stick or ½ teaspoon ground cinnamon

6 medium eggs

½ teaspoon bicarbonate of soda

1 teaspoon salt

40g melted butter or vegetable oil

yogurt, to serve

This large, thick omelette consists as much of green herbs as it does of eggs. It contains fresh fenugreek leaves, which are not always easy to find, although they are sometimes available from Asian grocers. A couple of tablespoons of dried fenugreek leaves (not seed) can be substituted if this is all you can find; otherwise, just increase the proportions of the other herbs.

Preheat the oven to 180ºC and line the base of a 20cm pie dish, or a cake tin with a fixed base, with a disc of greaseproof paper. Chop the parsley, coriander, dill, fenugreek and leek together fairly finely (an electric chopper comes in handy for this). Add the garlic to the mixture.

Grind the peppercorns, cumin, cardamom and cinnamon together in a grinder or using a mortar and pestle. Break the eggs into a large bowl and whisk in the spice mixture, bicarbonate of soda and salt. Stir in the chopped herbs.

Pour the melted butter into the base of the pie dish. Then pour in the egg mixture. Bake for 30–40 minutes until the mixture has completely set and is a little spongy.

Traditionally, a kuku is cooked in a large frying pan over a low heat. It should brown a little underneath before being turned. If you use this method, put a large plate over the pan, flip it and then slide the kuku back in so that both sides cook.

Drain the excess oil from the kuku, then cut it into wedges and eat hot, warm or cold with a little yogurt.

Nuray's Lentil and Bulgur Balls

Makes about 30/serves 6–8

180g red lentils

4 tablespoons tomato purée

100g bulgur wheat

100ml light olive oil or sunflower oil

1 onion, chopped finely

1 tablespoon finely chopped fresh dill

1–2 tablespoons finely chopped fresh parsley, to taste

dried chilli flakes, to taste

ground black pepper

2 garlic cloves, crushed

1 teaspoon salt

juice of 1–2 lemons, to taste

1 cos lettuce and green salad, to serve

This traditional dish is made by Turkish women to share among themselves at all-female parties. The Turkish friend who taught me how to make it is very particular about the texture, insisting that the bulgur should be a finely ground type. I make it using ordinary bulgur, which is easier to handle. I'm not sure it would pass muster with Turkish housewives, but it is good at a picnic, or as a cold nibble for a barbecue.

Put the lentils and 500ml water in a pan and bring to the boil. Cover and simmer gently for 15 minutes or until the lentils are cooked but still holding their shape – keep checking so that they don't overcook. Turn off the heat and stir in 2 tablespoons of the tomato purée and the bulgur. Cover and leave to one side for 1 hour.

Meanwhile, heat the oil in a frying pan over a medium heat and add a generous half of the onion. Stir and fry gently until it becomes transparent. Turn off the heat.

Tip the lentil mixture into a bowl. Stir in the fried onion with its oil, plus the remaining raw onion, and all the other ingredients except the lemon juice. Stir very well, taste and adjust the seasoning, adding lemon juice to taste.

Shape into walnut-sized balls. The mixture should hold together without being overly sticky or dry. Chill until needed.

Remove the leaves from the lettuce. Use each one like a little boat, putting four or five of the balls inside in a row. Serve with green salad.

PICNICS FOR SPECIAL EVENTS

This section opens with a few dainty nibbles and a cocktail intended for a punting picnic, but they can be adapted to serve as appetisers for more elaborate special occasion picnics. The idea of including such a picnic came from a friend's niece, studying in Oxford, although food appeared less important than alcohol in her descriptions of these.

This left plenty of scope. My imagination has always been caught by one of the most famous picnics in English fiction, that provided by the Water Rat in *The Wind in the Willows*, who loved messing about in boats and whose fat wicker luncheon-basket had 'cold chicken inside it… coldtonguecoldhamcoldbeefpickledgherkinssaladFrenchrollscress sandwichespottedmeatgingerbeerlemonadesodawater—'

The Rat was clearly a convivial fellow, an over-optimistic caterer who liked his food – and was also of his time. In a typically Edwardian way (the book was first published in 1908) his picnic is meat-heavy. We might prefer something lighter and less overwhelming. Below are some possible solutions to this, using the foods mentioned. They should, of course, be packed in a basket; one with a divided lid, hinged in the middle underneath the handle, is best. Put frozen ice packs in the base. It is finger food, so cutlery is unnecessary, but plates might be appreciated and glasses are essential. Take some fruit, soft drinks, water, and a flask of ice as well as napkins – I suspect the Water Rat owned some nice white damask ones – for wiping fingers.

The napkins, and much more, become essential when planning a full-blown special events picnic. So much depends on unknowables. The opera, the play or the music will be perfect, the firework display spectacular, the view quintessentially romantic in the proper 18th-century manner – if you can see it – and the weather, of course, will be glorious. Or will it? So the food is of great importance, because it may be the only thing that is actually fully under your control. This type of picnic demands the whole works: a beautiful cloth and napkins, the best cutlery, good china and crystal, a picnic rug and cushions to sit on, at the very least, or perhaps a table and chairs. And the food should both look and taste good. Choose from the dishes below to make a three-course menu of chilled soup, main course and dessert. Take extras, as felt to be necessary:

· Good wine, some sparkling water or other soft drinks.
· A flask of ice.
· Carefully selected cheese, a nice board to put it on, and a cheese knife.
· Biscuits and fruit to go with the cheese.
· Chocolates or petits fours if desired.

Bresaola Rolls

Serves 4

150g rocket leaves, torn if large

2 teaspoons olive oil

a few drops of balsamic vinegar

100g bresaola

30g Parmesan cheese, thinly shaved

6 medium pickled gherkins, cut
lengthways into 4

*Perhaps Ratty and Mole would rather have picnicked off rare roast beef, but these
are good as light appetisers with drinks for any occasion.*

Put the rocket in a bowl. Mix the oil with the vinegar in a small bowl and
use this to toss through the leaves. They should be very lightly coated.

Spread out the slices of bresaola and divide the leaves among them. Scatter
over the Parmesan, and put a sliver of gherkin in the centre of each pile.
Roll the slices firmly around the filling. Chill until needed.

These are small, lightweight and easily transported in a deep plate or box.
Put it on top of a frozen icepack to keep the rolls well chilled.

Lettuce Wraps with Chicken and Tongue

Serves 4

100g cold cooked chicken, roughly chopped

100g cooked tongue, roughly chopped

4 tablespoons mayonnaise

a pinch of chilli powder

3 small heads of little gem lettuce or white chicory

2 tablespoons capers, rinsed, drained and chopped

Another light appetiser for all sorts of events, and one that covers the chicken and tongue element of Ratty's picnic, these wraps use a mixture based on a 19th-century original — it also makes a good sandwich filling.

Put the chicken and tongue into a food processor, then add the mayonnaise and chilli powder, and blend together to make a paste.

Carefully remove the leaves from the lettuce or chicory. Select the nicest and most evenly sized. Put a teaspoonful of filling in the hollow of each leaf (there will be enough for about 24). Garnish with the capers. Chill until needed.

These need careful packing and are best in a single layer on a long dish, covered with clingfilm, and should be kept chilled during transit.

Ham in French Bread
with Watercress Butter

Serves 4

1 baguette
250g good-quality, thick-cut ham

For the watercress butter
100g watercress, coarse stalks removed
1 tablespoon lemon juice
1 teaspoon Worcestershire sauce
250g salted butter, cut into pieces

The Water Rat mentions cold ham, French rolls and cress sandwiches. Use a really good thick-cut, hand-carved ham to fill sandwiches made from a baguette spread with watercress butter. A full-length baguette and about 250g ham should be about right for 4 people. Use half quantities and make small, dainty pieces for appetisers and for special occasions.

To make the watercress butter, put all the ingredients in a blender or food processor and blend together to make a paste. Chill well until needed, and soften to room temperature before use.

Split the baguette lengthways and spread lavishly with the watercress butter, then pile the ham in thickly. Cut into short, diagonal lengths, then wrap the entire loaf tightly in greaseproof paper for transport.

It is not so important to chill this, and the flavour of the butter is better at room temperature.

Lemon Gin

Serves 1

3–4 ice cubes

25ml gin

25ml limoncello

25ml undiluted Lemonade (see page 37) or purchased lemon cordial

100ml soda water

lemon juice to taste, depending on the acidity of the cordial

a long strip of lemon zest, cut with a vegetable peeler, to decorate

The Water Rat is certainly partial to a beer or two in The Wind in the Willows. *How he felt about something stronger isn't clear, but the mention of lemonade and soda water, and ideas about summer cocktails, sparked off thoughts along the lines of the gin-based cocktail known as a Tom Collins.*

Put the ice in a 250–300ml highball glass. Add the other ingredients in the order listed and stir. You may wish to add a little lemon juice to achieve a pleasing sweet–acid balance; this depends on the type of lemon cordial used. Garnish with a strip of lemon zest.

For a picnic, mix the gin, limoncello and lemonade, then carry the ice in a flask and the soda water in a cooler or packed with ice packs, plus a lemon or two for the juice and garnish. You'll need a knife and a small board to cut the lemon on.

Salt Sticks

Makes about 35

200g peeled potato, boiled and mashed (without milk, butter or seasoning), cold

200g butter, softened, plus extra for greasing

200g plain flour, plus extra for dusting

1 medium egg, separated

1 generous teaspoon salt

seeds, such as caraway, nigella, cumin, sesame or poppy, for sprinkling

These sticks, worked up from a recipe given by Sir Harry Luke in his book The Tenth Muse, *have a delicate texture and are very moreish. They are excellent with aperitifs or soups.*

Preheat the oven to 170°C and lightly grease 3 baking sheets. Mix the mashed potato with the butter, flour, the egg yolk, and the salt. Chill for 30 minutes – this helps it to firm up.

Dust a work surface liberally with flour. Divide the potato dough into two pieces (it's easier to handle this way). Roll out each to a rectangle a bit less than 1cm thick and roughly 18 x 25cm. Neaten the edges if necessary.

Start at one of the shorter sides and cut into 16–18 strips. Whisk the egg white a little, brush the top of the sticks lightly with it and scatter with whichever type of seed you prefer. Using a spatula, carefully transfer each piece to a baking sheet.

Bake for 30 minutes, watching them closely for the final 10, until dark gold and cooked through. Cool on a wire rack and store in an airtight container.

Gazpacho Shots

Serves 4

400g of the best vine-ripened tomatoes you can find

1 red pepper, deseeded and cut into chunks

½ small cucumber, peeled and cut into rough chunks

½ red onion, roughly chopped

1 large garlic clove, roughly chopped

½ teaspoon salt

1 teaspoon sherry vinegar

20ml very good-quality extra virgin olive oil, or to taste

To serve
2cm piece of cucumber
1 small-medium tomato
a few chives
cracked ice
100ml chilled vodka

Serve this refreshing chilled soup-cum-cocktail as an appetiser on a hot summer's day. The tomatoes, peppers and onions we can buy in the UK are never going to have quite the same savour of those in Spain, but vine-ripened tomatoes are reasonably reliable. I've kept the amount of olive oil to a minimum, because in quantity it makes the drink filling.

Serve with a few little rolls of thinly sliced jamon serrano or jamon de bellota and Paprika Cheese Biscuits (see page 64).

Cut out the slightly woody core from under the stem of each tomato, then slice the tomatoes. Put all the vegetables into a liquidiser and blend well. Then pass the blended mixture through a sieve or food mill, reserving the juice and discarding any solids left behind.

Add the salt, vinegar and olive oil to the juice, stirring well. Taste and check the seasoning. Chill well until serving.

To serve: peel the cucumber, remove the seeds and chop in tiny dice. Drop the tomato in boiling water, drain and remove the skin. Discard the seeds and cut the flesh into tiny dice like the cucumber. Snip the chives into short lengths. Add a few lumps of cracked ice to each of the 4 glasses and divide the vodka between them. Fill up the glasses with gazpacho and top each one with a little of the cucumber and tomato dice, and a few of the snipped chives. If necesary, prepare the garnish in advance and add it to the drinks at the picnic spot.

Paprika Cheese Biscuits

Makes about 24

60g unskinned almonds
120g cold butter, cut into pieces
180g plain flour, plus extra for dusting
90g mature Cheddar cheese, grated
a pinch of salt
1 teaspoon paprika, preferably smoked
1 medium egg yolk

Fragile and delicious, these savoury biscuits are packed with flavour and make for elegant finger food.

Preheat the oven to 180°C. Put the almonds in a food processor and whizz until they are reduced to a coarse powder. Add the remaining ingredients and continue to process until they resemble coarse crumbs. Turn the mixture out onto the work surface and knead lightly until it forms a coherent dough. If it seems very soft, chill it for 20 minutes.

Dust the work surface with flour and roll out the dough to a thickness of just over 5mm. Cut into rounds using a 6cm biscuit cutter. Knead the scraps together and re-roll to make more biscuits.

Put onto baking sheets leaving a little space between each (they will spread slightly) and bake for 12–15 minutes until golden. Cool on a wire rack. These are best eaten on the day they are made, and to be carefully packed in a tin or plastic box before being transported.

Crème Vichysoisse

Serves 4

3og butter

350g peeled potato, cut into small pieces

3 leeks, white part only, sliced into 1cm pieces

150ml double cream

a little ground mace, to taste

milk (optional), as needed

salt and ground white pepper

chopped chives, to serve

This simple and delicious soup is useful for the unreliable British summer, because it is equally good served hot or iced. Carry in a preheated or chilled flask as appropriate and add the cream and a garnish of chives when serving.

Melt the butter in a large saucepan and add the potatoes and leeks. Cover and sweat over a low heat for 30 minutes or until soft. Add 500ml water and 1 teaspoon salt, and bring to the boil. Simmer for 30–35 minutes until the vegetables are well softened.

Remove from the heat and leave to cool a little, then use a blender or food processor to make a very smooth purée. Taste and add a little more salt if necessary, plus pepper and mace as desired. If the soup seems too thick, add a little water or milk to thin. If serving hot, reheat to boiling before transferring it to a flask. If serving cold, chill well. Add a generous swirl of cream and a scattering of chives to each portion as you serve the soup.

Pistachio Chicken

Serves 4

2 tablespoons sunflower oil or other neutral-flavour oil

1 onion, very finely chopped

1 bay leaf

1 teaspoon fennel seeds

600ml well-flavoured chicken stock

4 boneless, skinless chicken breasts, trimmed

salt

fresh tarragon or coriander leaves and a few pomegranate seeds, to garnish

Spiced Rice Salad (see page 68) and French beans (optional), to serve

For the garam masala
2cm piece of cinnamon stick
seeds from 8 green cardamom pods
1 teaspoon cumin seeds
12 cloves
1 teaspoon black peppercorns

For the garlic and ginger paste
4 garlic cloves
a thumb-sized piece of fresh root ginger, peeled and cut into chunks

For the pistachio paste
100g good quality unsalted, unroasted shelled pistachio nuts
4 mild green chillies, deseeded
1 green bird's eye chilli, deseeded
160ml single cream

Although this dish is mildly complicated to make, it can be prepared 12–24 hours in advance. Chicken breasts are easiest to cook and eat, but it could also be made with the meat from a whole chicken, jointed and partially boned before cooking. Serve with Spiced Rice Salad (see page 68) and some lightly cooked French beans tossed in a little oil and vinegar and chilled, or follow with a green salad.

Put all the ingredients for the garam masala in a small frying pan over a medium heat and heat for 1–2 minutes until they smell slightly roasted. Transfer to a spice grinder or mortar and pestle and grind to a powder. To make the garlic and ginger paste, blend the garlic and ginger together in a mini food processor, adding 1 tablespoon water if needed, until they make a paste. Tip into another bowl.

To make the pistachio paste, put the pistachio nuts in a small saucepan and cover with boiling water. Simmer for 5 minutes, then drain and rub them in a clean tea towel to remove the skins. Reserve 6 of the best for the garnish. Put the remainder of the nuts in a blender or food processor and add the chillies and cream, then blend to as smooth a paste as possible (I do them in batches using a wet-and-dry spice grinder).

Heat the oil gently in a frying pan over a low heat and add the onion. Cook until soft but not coloured. Stir in the garlic and ginger paste and fry for 1 minute, then add the pistachio paste. Stir until it is heated through, then add two-thirds of the garam masala, and the bay leaf, fennel seeds and 1 scant teaspoon salt. Pour in the stock and slide in the chicken breasts. Simmer gently for 15 minutes or until the chicken is cooked through. Remove the chicken to a serving dish.

The sauce should now be quite thick; boil it down a little if it is still on the thin side. Taste and add a little more salt and the remainder of the garam masala, if needed. Leave to cool to room temperature. If serving with rice, add to the plate in a border, then pour the sauce over the chicken, leaving the border of rice showing. Slice the reserved pistachios nuts, then garnish the chicken with a pattern made from herb leaves, slivers of nut and the pomegranate seeds. Chill until needed and serve cool if eating outdoors.

To transport, arrange in a dish about 3cm deep (a gratin dish is good) with clingfilm stretched over the top for transport. The sauce should set a little when cold. If in doubt, carry the chicken and rice in a clingfilmed dish, the sauce in a watertight container or screwtop jar, and garnish in a separate container; pour the sauce over and add the garnish just before serving.

Spiced Rice Salad

Serves 4

a generous pinch of saffron strands

1 onion, halved

150ml sunflower oil or other neutral-
flavour oil

a thumb-sized piece of fresh root ginger,
peeled and grated

200g basmati rice

½ teaspoon salt

1 tablespoon dried barberries or currants

50g almonds, blanched and halved

1 tablespoon lemon juice

freshly grated nutmeg

ground black pepper

Serve this cold rice dish to accompany the Pistachio Chicken (see page 66), or any grilled meats, or as part of a larger spread of dishes. The saffron is optional, but it makes a nice addition, as are the barberries, which are available from Middle Eastern grocers.

Grind the saffron using a mortar and pestle, then add 1 tablespoon hot water and leave it to soak.

Chop half the onion finely. Heat 1 tablespoon of the oil in the saucepan you intend to cook the rice in over a medium heat, and fry the ginger for 1–2 minutes until lightly golden. Add the chopped onion and cook gently until it is soft but not coloured.

Add the rice and salt, and stir well, then pour in 400ml water and the saffron water. Stir well, then cover tightly and bring to the boil. Turn the heat down to as low as possible and leave to cook very gently for 10–15 minutes until all the water has been absorbed and small holes appear on the surface of the cooked rice. Check after 10 minutes. When ready, fold a tea towel and put it across the top of the pan, then fit the lid over the top. Leave to steam very gently for another 10 minutes, then turn off the heat.

Slice the remainder of the onion very finely. Heat all but 2 tablespoons of the remaining oil in a small frying pan. Fry the barberries for 1 minute, then remove them with a slotted spoon and drain on kitchen paper. Do the same with the almonds, stirring until they turn golden brown. Remove these and drain as well.

Fry the sliced onion briskly, stirring frequently until soft. Turn down the heat and keep stirring and frying until the onions are chestnut brown and crisp. Remove them from the pan, drain and discard the oil.

Mix the remaining oil with the lemon juice and stir into the rice. Grind in some pepper, add a grating of nutmeg, then taste and check the seasoning. Transfer to a serving bowl or dish and garnish with the onions, almonds and barberries. If you don't want to serve it immediately, leave the ungarnished rice to cool, stirring occasionally, then cover and chill. Stir again before serving and scatter the garnish over the top.

New Potato, Asparagus, Spinach and Blue Cheese Frittata

Serves 6–8

350g new potatoes, scraped and cut into 1cm dice

200g asparagus, trimmed of any tough parts and cut into 2cm lengths

40g butter

3–4 spring onions, cut into short lengths

200g young spinach leaves

8 medium eggs

½ teaspoon salt

100–150g strong blue cheese, cut into small cubes

ground black pepper

This is a vegetarian main-course alternative for a posh evening picnic. (It can also be cut in wedges and used as part of a walker's pack-up, or served at a large family picnic.) The quantity of asparagus given here is a minimum; use twice as much, if you've got it. For the cheese, I tested the recipe with Swaledale blue, which has quite a powerful flavour, but you could experiment with any other blue cheese. Good bread and a green salad are best with this dish.

Boil the potatoes for 6 minutes or until not quite tender. Drain. Blanch the asparagus by putting it in a frying pan over a medium-high heat, pouring boiling water over it and just returning it to the boil. Drain and remove from the pan.

Melt 10g of the butter in the frying pan and cook the spring onions to soften without browning. Add the spinach leaves and turn them gently until they have wilted. Transfer to a large bowl.

Put the eggs in a large bowl and with the salt and a generous amount of pepper, then beat well. Add the potatoes and asparagus. Drain any excess liquid from the spinach and add the spinach to the bowl. Finally, fold in the blue cheese.

Melt the remaining butter in the frying pan over a low heat and, when it foams, pour in the egg mixture. Cook over the lowest possible heat for 15–20 minutes until the top is almost set. Cover with a lid to complete the cooking, or if this seems to be taking too long, put the frying pan under the grill for a few minutes. Be careful it doesn't burn.

This can be carried to the picnic in the pan it is cooked in or carefully turned onto a plate to cool, in which case cover with foil for transit.

Buttermilk Posset with Peaches and Redcurrants

Serves 4

400ml double cream
1 vanilla pod
200ml buttermilk
125g caster sugar

For the fruit purée
200g redcurrants
2 teaspoons sugar
2 small white flat or doughnut peaches

This is a fresh-tasting dessert where the cream is 'set' with buttermilk instead of the more usual lemon juice. The fruit purée is tart to contrast with the soft sweetness of the posset. Serve with Hazelnut Shortbread (see page 72).

To make the fruit purée, put the redcurrants in a saucepan over a low heat and cook gently until the juice starts to run. Bring to the boil, stir well, then remove from the heat and rub through a sieve to extract as much pulp as possible. Discard the seeds. Stir the sugar into the purée until dissolved.

Put the peaches in a bowl of boiling water for up to 1 minute (ripe peaches will take less time). Remove and cool under cold water. Use the tip of a knife to loosen the skin, then peel it off. Cut the peaches in half and remove the stones. Cut the flesh into small slices and mix with the redcurrant purée. Divide this mixture among 4 glasses (I use chunky tumblers which hold about 300ml) and chill.

Put the cream and the vanilla pod in a heavy-based saucepan over a low heat. Heat very gently until the cream comes to boiling point – about 15 minutes, if possible. (If it reaches boiling point quickly, turn off the heat and leave to infuse for the remainder of the time.) Remove the vanilla pod. (Rinse and dry it, then return it to the sugar jar for future use.)

Put the buttermilk in a heatproof bowl. Add the sugar to the cream and stir well to dissolve. Heat a little once more if necessary, to ensure the mixture boils. Immediately remove the pan from the heat and pour the cream mixture into the bowl containing the buttermilk. Stir well, then divide this posset mixture among the glasses. Chill for several hours. To carry, put the glasses over a chilled ice pack in a box or other container so that they will remain upright.

Hazelnut Shortbread

Makes 12 small biscuits

30g hazelnuts
60g plain flour, plus extra for dusting
60g cold butter, cut into pieces
30g sugar

Delicious little biscuits, good with creamy desserts or on their own with coffee.

Preheat the oven to 160°C. Put the hazelnuts on a baking tray and toast in the oven for 8–10 minutes, or until lightly toasted. Keep an eye on them, they shouldn't be deeper in colour than pale gold. Put the hazelnuts in a clean tea towel and rub off the skins, then grind the nuts in a food processor.

Add all other ingredients and mix briefly until they form a dough. Turn this out onto a lightly floured surface and form it into a short log about 2cm in diameter. Wrap in foil and put it in the fridge for 5 minutes to firm up.

Cut the dough into 12 equal slices and put on a baking tray. Bake for 12–15 minutes until firm but still pale in colour. Cool on a wire rack and pack in an airtight tin.

Fruit Salad in a Melon

Serves 4–6

100g caster sugar
1 large melon, such as a cantaloupe, honeydew or piel de sapo
soft fruit (150g of each type), such as strawberries and raspberries
150g white fleshed peaches
150g cherries
a slice of pineapple, weighing about 150–200g
50ml kirsch, maraschino or other fruit liqueur, or 1–2 tablespoons rosewater, to taste
double cream (optional), to serve

Melons were once considered terribly exotic, and the gardeners at grand country houses vied to grow the best. The shape of fruit in the special melon houses were echoed indoors by beautiful creamware 'melon' tureens on leaf-shaped plates. A fine ceramic tureen might be a bit too much on a picnic, but a real melon shell makes a good container. Choose your melon carefully, bearing in mind its shape, colour and skin markings. Buy the best soft fruit you can find and afford (use wild strawberries, not ordinary ones, if they are available), and a well-flavoured kirsch. This dessert can be prepared 12–24 hours in advance.

Make a syrup by combining the sugar and 100ml water in a small saucepan over a medium heat. Heat, stirring, until the sugar has completely dissolved and the mixture comes to the boil. Leave to one side to cool.

Wash the melon and dry it. Then carefully cut out a section to make a lid. This looks best if you allow your 1950s' suburban food fantasies to run free and stand the melon on one end (remove a small slice from underneath, if necessary, so that it doesn't fall over), and cut the top off in zigzag cuts. It helps if you start this process at a point that can be relocated, say where there is a colour change or slight blemish, because you need to be able to replace the top.

Scoop out and discard the seeds. Remove the soft flesh using a teaspoon or melon baller, leaving a good layer of the firmer flesh attached to the skin. Pour out any juice. Rub over the outside of the melon with a piece of damp kitchen paper to remove stickiness, then put it, and the lid, in the fridge to chill.

Prepare all the other fruit as necessary: hull the strawberries and cut them into halves or quarters if large. Put the peaches in a bowl of boiling water for up to 1 minute (ripe peaches will take less time). Remove and cool under cold water. Use the tip of a knife to loosen the skin, then peel it off. Skin and stone the peaches and cut into pieces about the size of the raspberries. Halve and stone the cherries. Remove any skin and core from the pineapple and cut the flesh into small cubes.

Mix the soft and stone fruit and pineapple together in a bowl. Select the nicest pieces of melon flesh (if you haven't used a melon baller, trim neatly) and add to the mixture. Add the sugar syrup and liqueur. Stir gently and chill well.

Put the fruit salad and its syrup into the melon and replace the top just before you want to serve it or pack it for travel. Keep well chilled in transit, and carry upright in a suitable waterproof container. It is best standing in a shallow bowl, in case of leaks. Take a small ladle to serve the fruit, and pretty dishes or bowls to eat it from. Serve with double cream if you like.

This can also be made for a larger party of 12–16 people, using a large watermelon for the shell. Include some of the flesh in the salad for its beautiful colour, and add a proportion of Ogen or Charentais melon into the mix. Triple the quantities of all the other ingredients.

BONFIRE NIGHT PICNIC

———

Bonfire Night is a great excuse for outdoor food in a different atmosphere. The idea of being out in the dark, the smell of smoke and gunpowder, and the noise and light of fireworks is intensely exciting for children, and for quite a lot of grown-ups as well.

As a child growing up on a West Riding farm, Bonfire Night always seemed very special. The hedges provided ample cuttings and dead wood for the fire, which was built in a spot that was suitably remote from any buildings and properly dark at night. There were special foods associated with this time of the year, including 'plot' or bonfire toffee – a hard, crunchy, buttery toffee – 'parkin pigs' and men cut out of ginger biscuit dough, and Parkin itself, a sticky oatmeal-based gingerbread (see page 79).

A Bonfire Night picnic needs to be warming and substantial, especially if it's expected to stand in for an evening meal. The Minestrone Soup suggested here is a meal in itself (Tomato, Red Pepper and Lentil Soup, page 84, is a good alternative). Some foods have acquired a status of 'traditional' to the event, especially jacket potatoes cooked in the embers of a bonfire (see Potatoes in Tin Cans, page 177, for a version of this). Sausages are also sometimes suggested for cooking over the fire, but the heat is too intense in the early stages, and everyone is too hungry to wait when it has died down. It's better to cook them over a barbecue or in the oven, and bring them out to eat with bread rolls and mustard or ketchup; alternatively, make Sausage Rolls (see page 31).

Sweet Potato and Cardamom Scones

Makes 8 large scones

300g self-raising flour, plus extra for dusting

2 sweet potatoes, total weight 500g

½ teaspoon salt

60g cold butter, cut into pieces

60g soft light brown sugar

the seeds from 4 cardamom pods, crushed

50ml milk, as needed

1 medium egg, beaten

butter, to serve

These scones have a warm, slightly spicy flavour, and a lovely pale orange colour, perfect for autumn. You can use pumpkin instead of the sweet potato, if you prefer, although the scones will have a yellower colour and the flavour will be less assertive.

Preheat the oven to 200ºC, and dust a baking sheet with flour. Bake the sweet potatoes for 35 minutes or until soft. Scoop out the flesh into a bowl and mash well – you should have about 300g.

Put the flour, salt and butter in a bowl and rub together using your fingertips until the mixture resembles fine breadcrumbs. Stir in the sugar, then add the sweet potato and the cardamom seeds. Gradually mix in the milk to make a soft, rather sticky dough.

Dust the work surface with plenty of flour. Roll out the mixture gently to about 2cm thick, using flour to prevent sticking. Cut into rounds using a 7.5cm biscuit cutter. Transfer to the prepared baking sheet and brush the tops with beaten egg to glaze. Bake for 20 minutes or until lightly golden on top.

These are best eaten soon after cooking, preferably warm with lots of butter.

Minestrone Soup

Serves 6–8

2 tablespoons olive oil

1 onion, chopped

1 carrot, coarsely diced

2 celery sticks, coarsely diced

1 leek, coarsely diced

2 potatoes, peeled and
coarsely diced

1 courgette, coarsely diced

½ fennel bulb, coarsely diced

leaves from the centre of 1 small cabbage,
finely sliced

1 garlic clove, crushed

200g tinned tomatoes

1.5 litres chicken or vegetable stock

3 sprigs each of parsley, thyme and basil
leaves chopped, or ½ teaspoon each of
dried thyme and basil

500g cotechino sausage, skinned and cut
into thick slices

200g tin cannellini or flageolet beans, or
green lentils, drained and rinsed

100g frozen peas

lemon juice (optional), to taste

salt and ground black pepper

freshly grated Parmesan, to serve

Here is a version of the classic Italian soup–stew: a broth made with beans, chunks of vegetable according to season and cotechino, a coarse-cut Italian boiling sausage. If cotechino is not available, use 250g ham cut into small pieces, or try chorizo instead, remembering that it will add both salt and a spicy note to the finished soup. The soup can be kept hot in a wide-mouthed flask (try it also for a picnic lunch on a long journey or a cold-weather walk). It's best served with some grated Parmesan and good bread or perhaps Cheese and Pesto Scones (see page 88).

Heat the olive oil in a large saucepan over a medium heat and add the vegetables and garlic in sequence, stirring well in between. Add the tomatoes and stock, then bring to the boil. Add a scant 1 teaspoon salt (the sausage is quite salty) and pepper.

Cover and simmer very gently for 1 hour. Add the herbs, cotechino and beans. Continue to simmer for another 15 minutes. Add the peas, return to the boil and simmer for 15 minutes.

Taste and correct the seasoning, then add a little lemon juice, if you like.

Like many soups, this tastes better when allowed to cool and reheated the next day. Add a little Parmesan to each serving.

Parkin

50g butter, plus extra for greasing

500g medium oatmeal

¼ teaspoon salt

½ teaspoon bicarbonate of soda

2 teaspoons ground ginger

500g golden syrup

3 tablespoons rum

1 tablespoon single cream

A northern version of gingerbread, Parkin is based partly or wholly on oatmeal and is a sticky and satisfying food. It is important to use medium oatmeal to achieve the correct texture, and it should be baked a couple of days before it is eaten.

Preheat the oven to 150ºC, then grease and base line a 24 x 24 x 5cm square tin. Mix the oatmeal, salt, bicarbonate of soda and ginger in a large bowl.

Put the butter and syrup in a small saucepan over a medium heat until melted, then stir in the rum and cream. Pour into the oatmeal mixture and stir well to combine.

Pour into the prepared tin and bake for 1½ hours or until the mixture feels set in the middle when pressed and is just beginning to pull away from the edges of the tin. Cool in the tin. Keep covered and store for 2 days before cutting into 24 pieces.

Lambswool

Serves 8

butter, for greasing

8 cooking apples, such as Bramley

2 litres apple juice

8 cloves

2cm piece of cinnamon stick

2 long strips of lemon zest, cut with a vegetable peeler

100g sugar, or to taste

freshly grated nutmeg, to serve

This old-English drink was originally made with ale and the pulp of roasted apples. It was popular in the 16th and 17th centuries; when Puck, in A Midsummer Night's Dream, refers to a 'roasted crab[apple] in a gossip's bowl', he is talking about lambswool. Evidently it was a drink for all kinds of social occasions — a 'gossiping' being the gathering of women at the birth of a child.

The drink is good as a pick-me-up at the end of a bonfire picnic or a long winter walk. I prefer it made with apple juice, because modern beers tend to be too hoppy to be pleasant with the sweet spices, and cider gives a slightly bitter and unpleasantly acid edge to the drink. If an alcoholic version is required, try adding rum or brandy to a juice-based one.

Preheat the oven to 180°C and lightly grease a baking tray with butter. Make a shallow cut around the circumference of each of the apples, then put them on the baking tray and bake for 30 minutes or until the flesh has cooked to a froth. Spoon out the cooked pulp, then discard the skins and cores. This stage can be completed 2 hours ahead, but no more than that.

Put the apple juice in a large saucepan with a lid. Add the spices and lemon zest, then cover and heat gently over a medium heat until it reaches a simmer. Turn off the heat and leave to infuse for 20 minutes. Strain into a jug and discard the spices and lemon.

Return the liquid to the pan and add sugar to taste, then stir to dissolve. Reheat gently to simmering point, then add the apple pulp. Blend with a stick blender to make a smooth mixture. Ladle into glasses and grate a little nutmeg over the top before serving.

PACKED FOOD FOR LONG WALKS

———

The British countryside offers enormous scope for walks, ranging from a morning or afternoon stroll on a summer day to challenging long-distance paths that take a week or more in whatever conditions the weather provides. Walking on a warm summer's day can be hot and thirsty work, in which a light lunch of a few sandwiches, plus some fruit and a bottle of water are enough. Crisp spring or autumn mornings, frosty winter days and unpredictable weather demand more and, although more challenging, they are often more fun and more rewarding; they provide better light and more interesting conditions for photographers, cooler walking (hot isn't always good) and a greater sense of reward generally – especially when one sits down to eat.

Soup is welcome on cold, raw days. Take well-wrapped sandwiches with moist fillings. As well as the suggestions in this section, see Pressed Sandwiches (page 101), and maybe hard-boiled eggs, perhaps with a little Dukkah (page 45), wrapped in a twist of paper to eat with them. Fruit is always good. If you are taking oranges – which are very thirst-quenching – peel and divide them into segments before setting off to reduce mess and chores for cold fingers.

A selection of small high-energy snacks is important. Anyone who has wolfed down their sandwiches in the car park and then piled up a mountain, only stopping to recover from nausea shortly after the start, will say what a mistake this is. Save the soup and sandwiches for the top, and nibble some Granola Bar or Flapjack (page 95) for short energy bursts (when walking one feels one has earned them). The idea of small treats at intervals is also an incentive for children. Some people arrange their walks around the locations of country pubs for liquid refreshment. By all means do so if you wish, but the ideas here are for the self-sufficient. Take bottled water, and hot drinks in flasks (don't add milk beforehand, carry it separately), or consider if there is the possibility of taking a tiny camping stove and a kettle to brew a drink on the spot.

Tomato, Red Pepper and Lentil Soup

Serves 8

2 red peppers
1 teaspoon cumin seeds
30g butter
2 garlic cloves, chopped
2cm piece of fresh root ginger, peeled and grated
1 large onion, chopped
½ teaspoon turmeric
a pinch of chilli powder
200g red lentils
2 x 400g tins of tomatoes
a pinch of sugar, if needed
100ml single cream (optional)
salt

Here is a warming soup for a cold day's hill walking. The recipe makes a large quantity of soup, but it can be frozen.

Preheat the grill. Put the red peppers on a baking tray and grill them until the skins are black. Remove from the heat and cover with a bowl. Leave until cool, then peel off the skins, halve and remove the cores and seeds, then chop the flesh roughly.

Meanwhile, put the cumin seeds in a dry frying pan and toast them over a low heat until they turn a slightly darker colour and smell toasted. Grind in a spice grinder or using a mortar and pestle.

Melt the butter in a large saucepan over a medium heat. Add the garlic and ginger, then stir-fry for 2 minutes. Add the onion and fry gently until it softens without browning. Then add the turmeric and chilli, stir well and leave to cook for 2 minutes.

Tip in the peppers, lentils and tomatoes, add 600ml water and a generous 1 teaspoon salt and bring to the boil. Simmer gently for 30 minutes or until the lentils are soft.

Leave to cool slightly, then use a stick blender to make a smooth, thick soup. Taste and adjust the seasoning, adding a pinch of sugar if it seems on the acid side.

Add the cream if you are eating this at home; otherwise, leave this out and put the soup in a pre-heated flask as part of a warming picnic lunch.

Sandwiches for Walkers

For walking, and especially hill walking, the best sandwiches have moist fillings between bread that doesn't offer too much resistance. Soft white or wholemeal rolls are good alternatives to sliced bread. Very crusty bread is better avoided. Butter helps to make the bread easier to chew, but it is unnecessary, even futile, with the tomato and anchovy filling given below.

There is a catalogue of tried-and-tested favourite fillings: ham and mustard, cheese and pickle, hard-boiled egg sliced with salad or mashed into salad cream or mayonnaise, variations on tinned sardines or tuna. Everyone's family has these in their repertoire, a legacy of the habits and routines of generations. Here are a few more unusual suggestions from the great back catalogue of early 20th-century British picnic ideas. Of course, they can be used on any other occasion as one's fancy dictates — for afternoon tea, other picnics, and for travelling.

Oriental Filling

Makes 4 rounds of sandwiches (or 20 tiny afternoon tea sandwiches if used in the same manner as Cucumber Sandwiches, see page 18)

150g full-fat soft cheese
6–8 dried dates, stoned and chopped
50–60g salted peanuts (not dry roasted), to taste, coarsely chopped
4 tablespoons single cream
½ teaspoon black peppercorns, coarsely crushed
8 slices of brown bread
softened butter, for spreading

This combination of peanuts, dates and cream cheese was originally suggested by Ambrose Heath in his book Good Sandwiches and Picnic Dishes *(1948). Use with brown bread to make an interesting sandwich for long walks and journeys.*

Put the soft cheese in a bowl and stir in the dates and peanuts. Add enough cream to make the mixture soft and spreadable.

Divide the mixture among 4 slices of buttered bread. Sprinkle a little of the black pepper over each portion. Top with the remaining bread, press together and cut in half diagonally. Wrap the sandwiches well for carrying.

Asparagus Filling

Makes enough filling for 6 rolled
sandwiches, or 8–10 sandwich rounds
for small triangular sandwiches, or 12
bridge rolls

500g asparagus spears
a little olive oil
4–6 tablespoons mayonnaise, as needed
1 small freshly baked wholemeal loaf
softened butter, for spreading
6 cooked asparagus tips (optional)
salt

*Fresh asparagus makes a delicious and delicately flavoured sandwich filling.
It might seem a little effete for a day out in the hills, especially if made into
rolled sandwiches, as described below, but it is actually a delicious alternative
to more conventional walker's fare. If the mood takes you, reserve 6 asparagus
stalks before making the filling and roll one into the centre of each sandwich.
This filling can also be spread between slices of brown bread and then trimmed
into little triangles without crusts, or used in Bridge Rolls (see page 32), each
one topped with a little grated Parmesan or some sieved hard-boiled egg yolk for
afternoon tea or less mobile picnics.*

Preheat the oven to 170°C. Snap off any hard or woody sections from the
asparagus (use these to flavour vegetable stock). Put the olive oil in a small
roasting tin and add all the asparagus spears and tips in a single layer.
Add a pinch of salt, then roast for 15 minutes or until the asparagus is
tender. Remove from the oven and leave to cool. Take out and reserve the 6
asparagus tips for rolling into the filling, if using.

Put the asparagus stalks and tips, and any liquid they have produced, into a
food processor and blend into a coarse paste.

Transfer to a small bowl and stir in enough mayonnaise to make a pleasant
texture. Taste and add a little more salt if needed. (You can use the filling at
this stage to fill sandwiches or bridge rolls as normal.)

To make the rolled sandwiches, chill the loaf for 2 hours. Take a bread knife
and dip it into a jug of boiling water, then dry it before using for cutting.
Cut off the bottom crust of the loaf, then cut slices as thinly as possible
working from the base of the loaf towards the top. Depending on the size
of the loaf, it will be possible to cut about 6 slices before you reach the top
crust when, however sharp the knife, the slices will begin to distort.

Spread each slice with a thin layer of butter and then trim off the crusts.
Divide the asparagus filling among the slices and put an asparagus spear, if
using, at the short end of each slice.

Carefully roll up the bread around the filling, trying not to allow cracks to
form in the bread. Secure each roll with a cocktail stick. Chill until needed,
then remove the cocktail sticks before either packing in a plastic box or
arranging on a plate, depending on the occasion.

Tomato and Anchovy Filling

Makes enough to fill 4 individual
bread rolls generously, cut in half for
serving

---

1 large beef tomato or similar, about 250g

6 anchovy fillets in oil, drained and
finely chopped

2 tablespoons full-fat crème fraîche

4 French rolls or other white bread rolls
with a firm crust and fine crumb

*This is a delicious and moist sandwich filling. Skinning the tomatoes is not
absolutely essential, but the flavours mingle better without the skins. It's
important to remove all the pulp around the seeds as this will make the filling
too watery if left behind. Extra thick double cream, clotted cream or crème
fraîche can be used, but the slight acidity of crème fraîche blends best with
tomato. This is a good filling for hollowed-out French rolls. It can also be used
as an element in Pressed Sandwiches, (see page 101), perhaps with some mild
softish cheese such as mozzarella.*

Put the tomato in a heatproof bowl and pour boiling water over to cover,
leave for 30 seconds, then drain and peel off the skin. Cut the tomato in half
and discard the core, seeds and surrounding pulp. Cut the flesh into fine
dice, put them in a sieve and leave to drain for 1 hour.

Stir the anchovy fillets into the drained tomato. Add the crème fraîche and
stir again.

Cut the rolls across the top and pull out some of the crumb to make a hollow
in each side, then spoon in the filling (don't overdo it so that it oozes out).
Squeeze the sides together, wrap tightly, and chill until needed.

Cheese and Pesto Scones

Makes 9 scones

225g self-raising flour, plus extra for dusting

a pinch salt

60g cold butter, cut into pieces

100g mature Cheddar cheese, finely grated

130ml milk or water, as needed

3 tablespoons Pesto Genovese (see opposite)

1 medium egg, beaten

These don't win prizes for an elegant shape – there is a bit of the free-form sculpture about them – but the flavour more than compensates, and they will be eaten rapidly. They are best when freshly baked but still good eaten cold. Take them on a picnic, eat with soup on a long, cold winter walk, or as a snack on a long journey. It you have a campfire or barbecue going, wrap them in foil and warm gently before eating.

Use a really good pesto – I'm fortunate in living near an Italian deli whose owner makes his own. If you can only buy industrially made versions, it's worth making some (see opposite), for a really intense flavour.

Preheat the oven to 200°C, and dust a baking tray with flour. Put the flour and salt in a bowl. Rub in the butter until the mixture resembles fine breadcrumbs, then mix in the Cheddar. Stir in enough milk to make a soft, slightly sticky dough.

Dust a work surface generously with flour and briefly work the dough. Cut into three equally sized pieces. Working quickly, gently roll or pat each piece out to give a rough square about 1cm thick. Try to make the pieces reasonably neat and of a similar size and shape.

Use the pesto to spread over two of the pieces of dough, and stack one on top of the other. Top with the third piece of dough. Press gently together and re-roll slightly to give a piece of just over 2cm thickness. Trim the edges a little if they are really untidy. Brush the top with beaten egg and then cut into 3 along the top edge and 3 along the side to make 9 pieces.

Quickly transfer each one to the baking sheet and bake for 15–20 minutes until well risen and golden. Cool on a wire rack.

Pesto Genovese

Makes about 125g

50g fresh basil leaves
15g pine nuts
1 garlic clove
½ teaspoon salt
30g freshly grated Parmesan
40ml olive oil, plus extra if needed
salt

One among many types of herb and nut sauces, pesto is worth making at home simply for the wonderful aroma released by the basil and the intense flavour. As well as an ingredient for the savoury scones, above, it has many other uses – eat it with vegetables grilled on the barbecue, use it as a spread (see page 101), or add it to Minestrone Soup (see page 78). An interesting version of pesto can be made with wild garlic leaves, something that can be foraged on walks during springtime (see page 185).

Put the basil in a food processor and add the pine nuts, garlic and salt. Process together, then add the Parmesan and process again.

Add the oil and process to make a thick, slightly runny paste. Taste, and add a little more salt if you like, or a little more oil to give a slightly runnier texture.

Savoury Chickpea Flour Cake

For 4–6

3 tablespoons sunflower oil or rapeseed oil, plus extra for greasing

120g gram flour (chickpea flour)

60g peas, shelled fresh or frozen

a pinch of sugar

1 tablespoon lemon juice

5–6 mint sprigs, leaves chopped

1 fresh green chilli, or to taste, deseeded and finely chopped

1 teaspoon cumin seeds

1 teaspoon coriander seeds

a pinch of fennel seeds

½ teaspoon black peppercorns

1 teaspoon salt

a pinch of ground turmeric

2 large garlic cloves

a thumb-sized piece of fresh root ginger, peeled and roughly chopped

1 small-medium onion, thinly sliced

To garnish and serve

a few fresh mint leaves

a few fresh coriander leaves

1 green chilli, deseeded

1 tablespoon desiccated coconut

lettuce leaves, cucumber sticks, cherry tomatoes and mango chutney, to serve

This cake is vegan, gluten-free, nutritious, filling and very tasty.

Preheat the oven to 150°C and grease a small cake tin. Spread the gram flour on a baking tray and toast in the oven for 30–40 minutes, stirring occasionally, until it turns a little darker and gives off a slightly nutty, toasted aroma. Keep an eye on it, as the flour burns easily. Transfer to a bowl and gradually stir in 350ml water to make a thick batter. Leave to rest.

Cook the peas in boiling water until tender. Drain, then mash them roughly and stir in the sugar and the lemon juice. Stir the mint leaves and chilli into the mixture, then leave to cool.

Put the cumin, coriander, fennel and black peppercorns in a dry frying pan over a low heat and dry toast, stirring until they turn a little darker and release a toasted aroma. Grind to a powder using a grinder or mortar and pestle. Add the salt and turmeric. Put the garlic and ginger in a blender or wet grinder with 2 tablespoons water and process to make a paste.

Heat the oil in a deep saucepan and add the onion. Cook gently for a few minutes until soft but not coloured. Stir in the garlic-and-ginger paste and cook for 2 minutes, stirring well, then add the spice mixture. Fry for 1 minute, and then stir in the chickpea flour batter. Keep stirring. It will thicken to a custard-like consistency. Cook gently, stirring constantly, until the mixture becomes quite sticky. It becomes quite heavy in the last stages and relatively difficult to stir, but keep going, otherwise it will be too soft as it doesn't thicken any more when it cools. It will take 10–15 minutes to reach the correct thickness.

Drop spoonfuls of half the mixture into the oiled tin. Divide the pea and herb mixture over the top of the chickpea mixture, then top with the remainder of the chickpea mixture, pressing it down well. Use a fork to roughen the top.

Chop the mint, coriander and green chilli together. Toast the coconut lightly in a dry frying pan over a medium heat, then stir it into the herb mix and press lightly on top of the mixture in the tin. Chill overnight before cutting into wedges.

Put each slice onto a lettuce leaf before packing it for carriage in a suitable container. Take with you the cucumber cut into sticks, some cherry tomatoes and a small container of mango chutney to eat with it.

Cornish Pasties

Makes 2 large pasties

150g lard plus extra for greasing
300g plain flour, plus extra for dusting
200g potato, peeled and chopped
100g turnip, chopped
60g onion, chopped
300g chuck or skirt steak, finely chopped
milk or 1 medium egg, beaten
salt and ground black pepper

At its best, the pasty is a wonderful traditional portable food, but sadly it has now become an industrialised snack for the long-distance traveller. When it is home-made with care, however, it becomes a delicious treat for an outdoor feast.

Preheat the oven to 200°C and lightly grease a baking tray. To make the pastry, put the flour and ½ teaspoon salt in a large bowl. Put the lard in the freezer for 20 minutes, then grate it into the flour. Using a fork, stir in 6–8 tablespoons cold water until the dough just begins to hold together. Bring the dough together into a ball and knead lightly for a few seconds. Wrap in clingfilm and chill for 30 minutes before using.

Put the vegetables into a large bowl and mix together well, and, in a separate container, season the meat well with salt and black pepper and stir.

Dust a work surface with flour and, working quickly, roll the pastry out to a little under 1cm thick, then cut two dinner-plate sized rounds.

Divide the vegetable mix between these, covering half of each circle. Likewise, divide the meat between the two, scattering it over the vegetables. Speed is essential – the pasties become difficult to handle if the pastry becomes warm at this stage.

Brush the edges of the pastry with water, fold each piece in half over the filling and crimp to seal the edges. Brush the pasties with milk or egg to glaze.

Bake for 25 minutes, then reduce the heat to 180°C and cook for a further 35 minutes until golden. Cool on a wire rack.

Shooter's Sandwich

Serves 4

500g fillet steak from the tail end

15g dried sliced porcini mushrooms (optional)

2 tablespoons olive oil

100g button mushrooms, sliced

1 part-baked ciabatta loaf

salt and ground black pepper

finger-food salad, to serve

For the herb marinade

4 tablespoons red wine

2 teaspoons balsamic vinegar

1 garlic clove, crushed

2 teaspoons finely chopped parsley

1 bay leaf, finely sliced

3–4 thyme sprigs, leaves only

3–4 marjoram sprigs, leaves only, chopped

2 tablespoons olive oil

Here is the ultimate sandwich, and one whose name suggests it must have been popular with parties of gentlemen out for a day on the grouse moor or deer stalking. The much simpler original for this recipe was given by Elizabeth David, who suggested it as a good idea for events such as moving house, another time when you might also need a picnic to hand. The fillet steak makes it an expensive choice, but it's good, and a real treat to eat on a long walk where you have a lovely view to enjoy at the same time.

Put the marinade ingredients in a shallow bowl and mix well to combine. Add the steak, and rub the mixture into it well. Put in the fridge and leave it to marinate for at least 2 hours and preferably 24 hours, turning it from time to time.

Put the porcini, if using, in a small bowl and cover with 100ml warm water. Leave to soak for 30 minutes, then drain and reserve the soaking water. Preheat the oven to 230°C.

Heat the oil in a frying pan or a small, shallow cast-iron dish over a medium heat. Add the button mushrooms and fry briskly, stirring from time to time, until they begin to brown slightly at the edges. Stir in the soaked porcini and their liquid.

If you have used a frying pan, transfer the mushroom mixture to an ovenproof dish. Lift the beef out of the marinade, rubbing off any debris, and lay it on top of the mushrooms. Season with pepper and a scant 1 teaspoon salt. Pour the marinade into the dish underneath the meat. Roast for 15–20 minutes until medium-rare or done to your liking.

Bake the ciabatta as instructed on the packet and leave to cool. Slice it in half lengthways and remove some of the crumb from each half to leave a hollow in which the steak will fit. When the meat comes out of the oven, lay it in one side of the bread and distribute the mushroom mixture over it. The cooking liquid should have reduced to a few tablespoonfuls (if it hasn't, reduce it some more by fast boiling over the hob).

Check the seasoning and adjust if necessary. Pour the liquid over the meat and mushrooms. Put on the top half of the loaf, pressing it down firmly to enclose the filling.

Wrap firmly in foil, clingfilm or greaseproof paper. Put a small board on top and weight lightly with a couple of tins. Leave for 5 hours, or overnight, then unwrap and cut across the sandwich in slices at least 1cm thick.

Rewrap the sandwich to carry, and take finger-food salad, such as cherry tomatoes or radishes, and perhaps a hip flask of something warming to accompany the sandwich.

Flapjacks

Makes 16

175g butter, plus extra for greasing
350g jumbo oats
a pinch of salt
175g soft light brown sugar
3 tablespoons golden syrup
100g dark chocolate (optional)

Everyone has their own idea of what constitutes a good flapjack – a classic walker's or traveller's snack. For me a flapjack should be relatively thick, small in proportion to depth, slightly chewy and taste distinctly of butter.

Preheat the oven to 180°C and grease and line a 20 x 20 x 2cm square tin with non-stick baking parchment. Take half the oats and process them in a blender or food processor until they are reduced to a coarse powder. Tip them in a bowl. Add all the remaining oats and the salt, and mix well.

Heat the butter, sugar and syrup in a small saucepan over a low heat until the butter is melted and the sugar dissolved. Pour into the oats and stir well to combine.

Tip into the prepared tin and level the top carefully, using the back of a spoon to press it down well. Make the surface as even as possible, especially along the edges and in the corners.

Bake for 20 minutes or until golden brown and slightly puffy, but check periodically to make sure the mixture is browning evenly. It should be evenly golden, bubbling a little have a wonderful nutty, buttery smell.

Leave to cool a little in the tin, then and cut into 4 along each side. Cool completely in the tin.

If using the chocolate, melt it in a heatproof bowl over a pan of gently simmering water, making sure the base of the bowl doesn't touch the water.

Pipe or drizzle the chocolate in lines back and forth across the pieces, or dip each one to coat half the top. Leave to set, and store in an airtight tin. These are best eaten within a day or two of baking.

Almond Granola Bars

Makes 12 bars

50g butter, plus extra for greasing

150g jumbo oats

100g marzipan

about ½ teaspoon salt

50g almonds, blanched and halved

30g pumpkin seeds

100g dried apricots, each one cut in 4–5 pieces

30g honey

These bars are another high-energy snack useful for long walks and camping trips. Making bars that stick together well is a challenge. I add (purchased) marzipan, which helps with this, but as formulae vary slightly from manufacturer to manufacturer, you may have to experiment a little with brands – I used Dr.Oetker's in my latest version. Any leftover marzipan can be cut into blocks, wrapped in non-stick baking parchment and frozen.

Preheat the oven to 180°C, and grease and line a 20 x 20 x 2cm square tin with non-stick baking parchment. Take half the oats and process them in a blender or food processor until they are reduced to a coarse powder. Tip them into a bowl.

Shave the marzipan into the thinnnest possible slices and rub it into the oats until it disappears. Add all the remaining oats, the salt, almonds, pumpkin seeds and dried apricots.

Put the butter and honey in a small saucepan and heat gently until the butter has melted. Pour into the oat mixture and stir well. Tip into the prepared tin and level the top carefully, using the back of a spoon to press it down well. Make the surface as even as possible, especially in the edges and corners.

Bake for 15 minutes or until golden brown and slightly puffy, but check after 10 minutes and turn the tin if the mixture is browning unevenly.

Leave to cool in the tin. While still slightly warm, cut into 2 along one edge and 6 along the other to make long, slender bars. Allow them to cool completely, and store any bars you haven't eaten in an airtight tin.

PICNICS ON THE ROAD

———

Food available for travellers has improved enormously since the days of stale, white bread sandwiches, a staple of post-war station buffets, kept too long on display and only available in a choice of industrial ham or industrial cheese filling. Despite the improved choice, I still prefer to make my own food – it's cheaper, tastes better and you know what's gone into it.

The best food for travelling can be eaten easily, preferably with the minimum of crumb drop. It should travel well without too much special packing, and it should be satisfying and delicious,whether it's intended for a car journey or a long train ride.

Something to drink, even if only bottled water, should also be to hand, or if travelling by car, plan a stop somewhere just off the road where one can stroll in pleasant countryside and either light a camping stove and make tea or buy comforting hot drinks.

Rather than relying on chocolate bars, take fruit in season – something that is easy to eat. Cherries are especially good in summer, plums in autumn and apples in winter. Alernatively, you could make a Banana and Stem Ginger Cake (see page 36) or some Almond Granola Bars (see page 96) or Flapjacks (see page 95).

Pressed Sandwiches

Makes 8 pieces/serves 2–4

1 part-baked ciabatta loaf

3–4 tablespoons pesto, such as Pesto Genovese (see page 89)

1 small handful of rocket leaves

100g Italian cooked ham with herbs, thinly sliced

100g Gorgonzola dolce, rind removed

These sandwiches are known to my family as 'motorway sandwiches', because they are a favourite choice for long car journeys, but don't restrict them to this. They are great for country walks or picnics. In fact, they are good for anywhere where you might need a delicious, densely flavoured sandwich. (Shooter's Sandwich, see page 94, is made in a similar way, and is also worth considering for a long journey, especially one that involves a scenic lunch spot.)

Ingredients need to be chosen carefully to give a filling with a pleasant balance of the relatively salty and relatively mild, and a moisture content that both helps to hold the sandwich together and makes it good to eat.

Bake the ciabatta as instructed on the packet and leave to cool. Cut the loaf in half lengthways. Spread the cut sides with pesto. Distribute the rocket leaves over the base, followed by the ham.

Layer the cheese in slices over the ham, then put the top on the loaf and press lightly with your hand so that everything sticks together.

Wrap tightly in clingfilm, foil or greaseproof paper, as snugly as possible. Put the whole thing in the fridge overnight, preferably between two boards or plates with a small weight on top such as a tin of tomatoes.

Next day, unwrap the sandwich, leaving the sandwich on top of the wrapping, and carefully cut it into eight diagonal slices. Rewrap tightly. Remember to take a few pieces of kitchen paper for greasy fingers and in case of spills.

The sandwiches can be made in individual ciabatta rolls instead of one long one. Wrap them separately, and tightly, in cling film. As long as this is done tightly, pressing is not essential. A baguette can be used instead of the ciabatta although it makes more crumbs and is harder to chew.

Experiment with alternative fillings, remembering the principle of something to spread on the bread, a little salad, and two main ingredients that complement each other. Other possibilities for spreads include Tapenade (see below), spread thinly, Avocado Salsa (see page 144), a little French dressing or butter, or a sprinkle of olive oil.

· Watercress, sliced hard-boiled egg and Avocado Salsa (see page 144)

· French dressing, rocket, spianata Romana (a very spicy salami) or thinly sliced chorizo and a mild cheese such as Toma Piemontese.

· Tapenade (below), cold chicken, avocado and thinly sliced tomato.

Tapenade

Makes about 125g

75g black olives with stones
25g capers, drained
2 anchovy fillets
1 garlic clove
4 tablespoons olive oil
1 tablespoon lemon juice
1–2 teaspoons brandy (optional), to taste
leaves of 2 basil sprigs (optional)

My tapenade recipe from comes from the Languedoc. It is salty and powerfully flavoured, and you will find that a little goes a long way. As well as being a good spread in sandwiches, tapenade can be used as a dip to accompany vegetable crudités, and it also goes well with eggs, fish and vegetables. Don't be tempted to use ready-pitted olives because where you have no pits you also have no flavour. The brandy and basil are not essential but they help to mellow and lift the sauce.

Using a small sharp knife, cut the flesh off the olives, discarding the pits. Put all the ingredients in a blender or food processor and whizz to make a thick paste.

Feta, Mint and Courgette Muffins

Makes 8 large muffins

80g butter, melted, plus extra for greasing

200g courgette

275g self-raising flour

½ teaspoon salt

a pinch of dried chilli flakes

200g feta cheese, crumbled

1 handful of fresh mint leaves, coarsely chopped, or a generous 1 teaspoon dried mint

2 medium eggs, beaten

175ml milk, as needed

These savoury muffins are good for journeys and picnics generally. Take a few cherry tomatoes to eat with them. I found some miniature moulds made out of paper, which made loaf-shaped muffins. They made a nice change from the more regular round ones.

Preheat the oven to 200°C and line an 8-cup muffin tin with paper cases or put 8 small paper loaf moulds on a baking sheet. Brush the inside of the cases with a little melted butter.

Grate the courgette coarsely. Put it in a clean tea towel and wring hard to extract as much liquid as possible.

Put the flour, salt and chilli flakes in a bowl. Add the feta, mint, butter, beaten eggs and courgette, and mix well. Gradually add the milk and stir in until the mixture has a dropping consistency.

Fill the cases to about two-thirds full. Bake for 25–30 minutes, or until a cocktail stick inserted into the centre comes out clean. Eat warm or cold.

Using Fire

Lighting a fire for cooking takes outdoor food into a new dimension and is another element in the unpredictable adventure of eating al fresco. A picnic is artifice; a campfire is survival – or so we like to think. Barbecues lie somewhere in between, surrounded by glamour derived from North American influences and all the accessories that are deemed necessary. The combination of managing naked flames and the potential for collecting odd-shaped implements is remarkably appealing to people who might otherwise take no interest in cooking.

You don't need to be camping in the sense of living outdoors to light a campfire – follow the example of previous generations and light one to heat one or two ingredients to go with the remaining meal. The smell of wood smoke, the crackle of the flames and the heat (especially if the day is on the chilly side) add another aspect to a meal outdoors. Barbecues are designed with the specific purpose of grilling food, although the heat can also be used for cooking all kinds of other things. I sometimes put pans of water on the grill for boiling eggs or other foods, and as long as heat control is not crucial, this works fine. Campfires, with careful management, produce a range of heat, from the blazing hot to the very slow, and, given suitable implements and containers, you can cook anything from grilled marshmallows to large and complex stews on them.

National Trust properties try, where possible, to encourage campfires or barbecues, but policy varies and often it is only permitted in particular areas at properties. Always ask staff at individual locations, check local signs and follow the Countryside Code, a guide to enjoying the countryside generally, in a manner that recognises the responsibilities and safety of visitors and inhabitants alike. It can be viewed at the Nature England website (see page 208).

National Trust properties that encourage barbecues in areas provided include Studland (Dorset), Clumber Park (Nottinghamshire), Bossington (on the Holnicote Estate, Somerset) and Lyme Park (near Stockport, Cheshire). Lighting fires generally is often discouraged by landowners and campsites, however. There are problems with safety, the possibility of fire spreading to crops or other vegetation, and the potential for irritating other people with smoke. Some campsites have begun to provide fire pits. Rules relating to Areas of Outstanding Natural Beauty, National Parks, Ancient Monuments and Sites of Special Scientific Interest all have a bearing on the use of barbecues and especially campfires, as do the attitudes of individual landowners and their tenants. Take local advice.

Beaches provide some of the best outdoor venues for al fresco barbecues and campfires. They often have pieces of driftwood – and a fire needs fuel. Always make sure that the smoke generated will not irritate anyone else and that there are no fire risks close by, and also be sure to extinguish all the embers afterwards, by pouring water over them if necessary. If you insist

Left The essential kettle for tea around the campfire.

on using a disposable barbecue, take the remains away and dispose of them properly. Anything that requires the digging of a pit, or special constructions for holding whole animals in place, is outside the scope of this book (delicious though clam bakes and hog roasts can be). Nor is this a manual of bushcraft or survival techniques. The ideas and recipes for cooking on a campfire are simple and rely on ingredients easily available from local shops, with some suggestions for a little modest foraging. It's more important that the recipes are interesting, fun, and most of all, produce good food.

Food hygiene

Everyone has tales of barbecue food from hell: sausages charred on the outside and raw in the middle, and chicken pink at the bone. The potential for food poisoning is real, and badly cooked food is unpleasant as well as dangerous. Take extra care over storing food. Cover dips and cold dishes with clingfilm, or put them in lidded boxes or bowls. Keep them in the fridge or a chilled cool box until needed, and keep them separate from uncooked food, especially meat and fish. Raw meat and fish should be stored in the fridge on lower shelves than salads or other prepared or cooked foods, or in separate cool box. Meat benefits from being given 20–30 minutes to reach room temperature before cooking, so remove it and allow it to stand, covered and out of the sun, for a short while when needed.

For cooking on a barbecue, it is important when cooking meat and fish to have hot enough coals – the white ash stage is crucial. Very hot coals will cook small pieces of food, such as fish, burgers, and steaks quickly, but some items, including sausages and especially larger pieces of meat, need longer cooking at a more gentle temperature. Get the fire started well in advance and allow plenty of time – more time than you think you need. Have a supply of dips and other nibbles for people to eat while things are cooking. Use a temperature probe to check the internal temperature of large pieces of meat, but the best way to discover if something is done is to cut it open. If it isn't cooked, put it back to cook a bit more.

There is a lingering misapprehension, perhaps to do with the initial burst of heat, that barbecuing is a quick method of cooking. Although it is true that small items will cook in minutes, they would also do so in conventional grills as well. Intense heat from embers, whether in a barbecue or campfire, browns the exterior of food very quickly, but heat penetrates to the centre more slowly, so try to keep anything that needs a while to fully cook through away from the hottest part of the coals to a less intense part of the fire. Don't worry that the food will lack the barbecue flavour – it will develop perfectly well over time. Be patient, allow plenty of time for cooking.

For large hunks of meat, use a kettle barbecue or any barbecue with a lid that has a generous amount of space underneath. Arrange the coals so that they are not directly under the meat and put a foil tray in the space left. This catches drips and fat so that it doesn't fall directly onto the coals and create too much smoke (some water can be added to the tray to prevent the drips drying out and burning).

Barbecued food, delicious as it is, benefits from sauces to help it go down. Make some flavoured butters or sauces such as pesto (see pages 89 and 185) and Tapenade (see page 102) to eat with it and also have some mayonnaise (a good-quality version bought from a shop is fine if you don't want to make it). Add a green salad dressed with oil and vinegar. For carbs, I prefer bread, but add in a potato salad (see page 41) or rice salad (see page 68), or your favourite couscous, tabbouleh or pasta salad.

Fire safety

Safety and courtesy should always come first, especially if you are planning to make a fire on land not belonging to you. Campsites usually have rules about lighting fires, although some provide purpose-built fire pits or barbecue pits. Always find out what the rules are before lighting anything. Lighting will involve a certain amount of smoke, so think about the comfort of others who might be nearby.

Away from organised outdoor facilities, choose a site carefully, bearing in mind the wind speed and direction, and the nature of the surrounding vegetation. An open space with some bare ground (a beach, lake shore or riverbank, for example) offers good possibilities. Don't light barbecues or fires in places where there is a lot of dry vegetation generally, or heather, peat and conifers, particularly plantations of pine, fir and the like. All these have the potential to literally go up in flames, and you do not want to be responsible for a forest fire. When you have finished with the barbecue or fire, make sure it is fully extinguished – the only sure way to do this is to pour water over the embers, as stated above.

Barbecue design

The design of a barbecue makes a huge difference to the way it functions and how food cooks. A basic barbecue can be acquired for a few pounds (in the past I've even improvised one using a bit of terracotta land drain, some crumpled chicken wire and a small piece of metal grille).

Barbecues are available in a bewildering variety of sizes and designs. All have pros and cons, some of which are outlined below. This still leaves enormous choice. Strangely, there seems to be a shortage of the most useful shape – a rectangular trough often improvised by cutting an oil drum in half. The length allows for a hot end for quick cooking and starting things off, and a cooler end for slow cooking, finishing items, and keeping food warm. A lid is helpful, and should be high enough to accommodate a whole chicken or a larger joint of meat on large barbecues.

Hibachis are small, shallow, tray-like barbecues, based on a Japanese design. They can be used in tiny spaces, and have two or three levels, but they only have space for relatively small items. They are useful in a restricted space and for cooking for small numbers, or for foods that need quick heat and a short cooking time, such as satay.

Bucket barbecues are the best choice if you want something portable, because these often have clip-on lids and carrying handles. They are easy to pack for a barbecue away from home, as part of a picnic or to take on a camping trip, and they can be used in small spaces. They are best for small items such as fish, steaks or sausages, or for cooking small amounts of something such as vegetables while a larger barbecue is being used for meat. Disadvantages include no choice of levels and difficulty in controlling the heat because of the restricted space, although coals could be moved between this and another suitable metal container using a pair of charcoal tongs.

Kettle barbecues come in many sizes, from that of a large bucket up to something that can accommodate an entire turkey. The largest allow enough space for keeping hot coals at one side, and sometimes have a rack for keeping food warm at a level well above the coals. Their domed lids make them good for big pieces of meat, whole chickens and long cooking, and the bigger ones provide large grilling areas, useful for cooking for bigger parties. They have the disadvantage that a bit of practise is needed to get the best out of them, and that the coals are sometimes relatively distant from the food.

Lighting a barbecue

As far as I'm concerned, barbecues are about grilling over charcoal (or the embers of a wood fire), which gives a great combination of heat and flavour. I acknowledge the existence of gas-fired barbecues, and I can see that they might be useful for large parties. I am ambivalent about briquettes, which give a sustained heat and have their uses for long cooking. And, on the subject of flavour, fire-lighters and lighting fluid give a chemical smell to fuel (although I admit that instant-lighting bags of charcoal work quite well).

The easiest method for lighting charcoal is to use a chimney starter. These are invaluable. They can take a batch of charcoal from a smouldering start to the white-ash stage in about 20 minutes, at which point the coals can be emptied into the barbecue proper to use almost immediately or to seed a fire with more charcoal if necessary. You simply put a couple of coils of newspaper (see below) into the base of the chimney starter and fill the top part with charcoal, then light the newspaper. If you've underestimated the amount of charcoal needed, or want to boost a low fire, simply light another batch of charcoal in the starter.

Left A newly lit campfire is a cheering sight; let it burn down before cooking begins.

Pine cones, egg boxes and newspaper are also invaluable fire-starting materials. Very dry, resinous pine cones may not need much beyond a match to get them started, especially if you have some dry pine needles to act as tinder (but see the safety notes above, and be very cautious indeed about starting fires anywhere near conifers). Three or four cones jammed into the base of a chimney starter will help it burn up well.

Some people sneer in a bushcraft kind of way at using newspaper to start barbecues and campfires, but if the aim is to cook food rather than demonstrate your knowledge of survival techniques, then why not? Start at a corner and roll a sheet into a long, reasonably tight roll, then tie the roll in a loose knot. Make several of these and tuck them down among the kindling or coals then set light to a couple of ends. If you have some pine cones handy, put one in the middle of each knot.

Alternatively, use an egg box. Put a lump of charcoal or a pine cone in each depression, close the top and bury it in the kindling or charcoal. Set light to one corner. And, when using matches, try to make sure you have extra-long cook's matches, then strike two together – doing this makes them less likely to get blown out by a puff of wind. Never use a barbecue indoors or in an enclosed space.

The state of the coals

Once the charcoal is lit and the initial smoke has died down, the coals need to burn until they are uniformly covered with white ash. This is essential. Keep an eye on them to make sure that they burn evenly and, especially in the early stages, that they don't go out. They can be gently moved with tongs to help distribute the fire evenly, but don't fiddle with them too much. Once the white-ash stage is reached, spread the charcoal to provide a suitable area for grilling over. Initially they should contain a lot of heat and will char things very fast, so it might be an advantage to have fewer coals – and therefore a cooler area – at one side of the barbecue.

If the coals seem to cool off, then it's useful to have a device known in my household as a wafter: something with which to fan the coals. A flexible round rush place mat works very well. Held halfway down using both hands and played vigorously over the coals, it can revive a sluggish fire in a surprisingly short time or induce a burst of heat to help brown the exterior of a slightly pallid piece of meat. Should a drip of fat land on the coals and ignite, a single, sharp flap towards you with the wafter is usually enough to blow out the flame.

Useful things

Many of the general observations about the practicalities of picnic food apply here too, especially if you're going to take a barbecue out for the day or on a camping trip, but there are some things that are specific to cooking over embers.

Use wire baskets to hold fragile foods and tongs to turn things. Brush items likely to dry out, such as very lean meat with oil or melted butter before and during cooking; some marinades can be used to brush items during cooking as well, but if raw meat or fish has been marinating in the mixture, only use this at the start of cooking. Alternatively, brush with a favourite barbecue sauce, or sprinkle the cooked side of meats with seasoning mixtures of herbs, spices and salt. The general advice is not to salt meat until the end of cooking, although I don't always follow this. Mediterranean cultures add extra flavour to meat and fish by adding rosemary branches or fennel stems to the coals, to create aromatic smoke.

Useful accessories for barbecuing include:
- Long-handled charcoal tongs and a poker or rake for moving hot coals around.
- Foil trays for catching drips under large, long-cooked foods.
- Tongs for turning pieces of food and moving them to hotter or cooler spots.
- Gauntlets and other oven cloths for protecting your hands from the heat.
- Brushes for adding oil or marinades. Pastry brushes can be used, or, for brushing food during cooking, make a bundle of herb sprigs – thyme, marjoram and rosemary – then tie it to a stick and use this instead.
- Washable metal or plastic trays for holding raw ingredients, and attractive ones for handing round nibbles and drinks.
- Different types of skewer: metal ones with a flat section for kebabs; double ones like giant hairpins for pieces of vegetable; small wooden ones for satay and other little delicacies (soak wooden ones for 30 minutes before using).
- Wire baskets for holding fragile food, especially fish, or for cooking batches of sausages, burgers or kofta.
- A digital probe thermometer – helpful for checking the internal temperature of poultry.
- Zip-type bags for marinating meat, especially if cooking away from home, and for holding batters and dry mixes when camping.
- Extra space – try to arrange some table space near to the barbecue.
- Lots of kitchen paper for wiping greasy fingers and generally mopping up.
- A wire brush for cleaning off the barbecue grill in between batches of food and after cooking.

Most of all, any barbecue chef needs a willing helper. There is always a point when another pair of hands is useful, or someone needs to be taking care of the food on the grill while you heat something else, pour drinks or greet guests.

AN EASY AND DELICIOUS
BARBECUE FOR FOUR

———

An ideal barbecue for a small group of friends, this is a selection of delicious little morsels that can be prepared a few hours ahead and need relatively minimal cooking. Carefully packed in a cooler, the items listed here could be taken to a beach or beauty spot, or you could just stay at home and eat in the garden. You'll need a small barbecue with medium-hot coals ready at the point of cooking.

Good accompaniments for the recipes in this section are bread, Potato Salad (see page 41), and your favourite green salad. Buttermilk Posset with Peaches and Redcurrants (see page 71) or Fruit Salad in a Melon (see page 72) are nice alternatives for dessert. A simpler option is a selection of well-chosen cheeses and a basket of summer fruit.

Grilled Quail

Serves 4

8 quail
juice of 1 lemon
3 tablespoons olive oil
coarse sea salt
good bread, to serve

Quail make good, simple barbecue food and cook quickly over medium-hot charcoal. For a more complex marinade, see page 94.

The quail can be cooked whole, or they can be prepared as follows: Cut through the backbone of each quail and press down with the heel of your hand on the breastbone to flatten the bird. Squeeze a little lemon juice over either side of each bird and sprinkle with oil (or use the herb marinade). Leave the birds for anything between 30 minutes and 4 hours. Put them in the fridge if leaving them for longer than 1 hour, and allow them to come to room temperature for 30 minutes before grilling.

When ready to grill, put each flattened bird on the barbecue grill so that the inside, containing all the bones, is closest to the fire. Cook for 4–6 minutes, depending on the heat, then turn and cook the skin side for about the same time. Lift each one using the tongs and allow the part where the meat is thickest to cook along the edge if necessary. Make sure the birds are cooked through, and brush with a little more oil as they cook. Alternatively, grill the birds whole, turning frequently until done.

Sprinkle with a little more lemon juice, add a scatter of coarse salt, and eat with good bread. Make sure you have plenty of kitchen paper or napkins for wiping greasy fingers.

Prosciutto-wrapped Scallops

Serves 4, as an appetiser

1 tablespoon oil

1 tablespoon lemon juice

1 tablespoon chopped herbs, such as chervil, parsley, tarragon, either singly or in combination

16–20 small scallops, depending on size, without the coral

80g prosciutto crudo

People will eat as many of these scallops as you are prepared to cook. An excellent little appetiser, they also make good hot canapés for a smart picnic or barbecue.

The packs of small scallops sold in supermarkets are ideal for this. If the only scallops available are large ones, which can be very expensive, buy just 1 per person and add some other appetisers (you may want to do this anyway) or choose alternatives – Bresaola Rolls (see page 56), Chilled Cucumber Cream (see page 42), Marinated Barbecued Prawns (see page 163), Salt Sticks (see page 61) and serve with various dips.

Soak 4 bamboo skewers for 30 minutes before cooking. Put the oil, lemon juice and herbs in a large bowl and mix well, then add the scallops. Leave to marinate for 30 minutes.

Remove the scallops from the marinade and wrap each in a piece of prosciutto. Thread onto the skewers and grill over hot coals for 4–5 minutes, turning frequently so that the prosciutto crisps and the shellfish cooks evenly.

If serving as canapés, slide the scallops off the skewers and put a cocktail stick in each one before serving.

Small scallops are also very good on skewers with a thin slice of chorizo in between each one. Grill them for 5 minutes, turning frequently.

Chicken Satay

Makes 12 appetiser-sized skewers

600g boneless chicken meat from the breast or thigh, cut into 1cm cubes

thinly sliced onions fried in oil until brown and very crisp (optional), to garnish

For the marinade
1 small onion, thinly sliced
2 garlic cloves, crushed
1 tablespoon soy sauce
a pinch of cayenne pepper
1 teaspoon ground coriander
1 teaspoon ground ginger
a squeeze of lemon or lime juice
1 tablespoon sunflower oil

For the sauce
1 tablespoon sunflower oil
2 shallots, halved and thinly sliced
2 garlic cloves, crushed
cayenne pepper, to taste
120g crunchy peanut butter
1 teaspoon Thai fish sauce
1 tablespoon lemon juice
1 teaspoon soft brown sugar

My version of the classic Indonesian dish is made with ingredients I had to hand at the time, which were not especially Indonesian, but it still produces something very acceptable. The sauce can be made the day before and reheated gently.

To make the marinade, put all the ingredients in a bowl and mix well. Put the chicken in the marinade and stir to coat. Put in the fridge and leave for at least 2 hours and preferably 24 hours.

Soak 12 wooden skewers in water for 30 minutes before cooking. To make the sauce, heat the oil in a frying pan over a medium-low heat, and add the shallots and garlic. Cook gently for 3 minutes, then add the cayenne and 250ml water. Stir and bring to the boil.

Add all the other ingredients, stir, then simmer quite briskly, stirring constantly until the sauce has become thick and creamy in texture (although the crunch of the peanut will still be apparent).

Divide the meat among the skewers, packing it fairly loosely onto the ends. Cook on the barbecue grill over a high heat, turning once or twice until the chicken is thoroughly cooked all the way through.

Reheat the peanut sauce and put it in a bowl, sprinkle over the fried onions to garnish, if using. Serve alongside the chicken for everyone to help themselves. If you plan to eat away from home, the sauce will need to be reheated over the barbecue, so put it in a small saucepan.

Strawberry and Muscat Wine Jelly

Serves 4

250–300g strawberries, hulled
4 tablespoons caster sugar
4 sheets (4g) gelatine

For the wine jelly
250–300g strawberries, hulled
4 teaspoons caster sugar
4 sheets gelatine
375ml well-flavoured dessert wine
(such as Brown Brothers Orange
Muscat and Flora)

ice cubes

This is an elegant, refreshing, and delicious dessert for a special barbecue or picnic on a warm summer evening. Make individual portions in glasses — you may want to use fairly chunky ones if you have to carry them any distance, and remember, if driving, that wine, even in a jellied form, still contains alcohol.

Cut the first 300g or so strawberries in pieces and put in a saucepan over a medium heat with 2 tablespoons water and the sugar. Heat gently, stirring, until the mixture comes to a simmer and the strawberries soften slightly and give up their juice. Don't cook any longer than necessary.

Put the mixture into a blender or food processor and blend to make a purée, then sieve the mixture over a bowl. Discard the pips.

Soak the gelatine in cold water to cover until it softens, then squeeze to extract as much water as possible. Return the strawberry juices to the pan, add the gelatine and heat gently until the gelatine has dissolved. Leave to cool a little before transferring to the glasses. Carefully divide among 4 glasses (I use chunky tumblers that hold 300ml). Chill until set.

To make the wine jelly, cut the reamining strawberries into halves or quarters, depending on size. Put in a bowl and sprinkle over the sugar, then leave to macerate for 1 hour.

Put the gelatine in a bowl and cover with half the wine. Leave to soak until soft.

Put the remaining wine in a small saucepan over a medium heat and heat gently. Add the gelatine and the wine it has soaked in, and stir until it dissolves. Don't heat any more than necessary.

Divide the macerated strawberries and any juice they have produced among the glasses. Take 4 tablespoons of the wine jelly mix and stir it in a small bowl over ice until it is at the point of setting, then divide among the glasses (this will help prevent the berries floating). Chill while the remaining jelly cools until nearly set. Divide this among the glasses, and chill again until needed.

A CYPRIOT-INFLUENCED BARBECUE

———

My husband's family learnt the art of barbecuing when they lived on the island of Cyprus in the late 1960s. They have strong feelings about how the event should unfold: a blazing-hot afternoon, a leisurely pace, a series of morsels delivered at intervals from the hot coals, eaten with cabbage salad and interspersed with refreshing slices of orange, plus an overwhelming quantity of crisps and other salty snacks and copious amounts of wine or fizzy soft drinks.

No one has told the British weather about this, and we sometimes find ourselves rigging up temporary covers for the barbecue and then retreating indoors with plates and glasses. I prefer a selection of dips, crudités and barbecued vegetables to an abundance of crisps, and I like to offer a few alternatives to all the alcohol and sugary drinks sold in the name of quenching thirst.

Skordalia (see page 28), Avocado Salsa (see page 144) and Sweet Pepper Relish (see page 148) are all good here. Select from the vegetable ideas below, and also have ready some really good sausages, or some marinated lamb chops or steaks (see Marinated Steaks page 154 for a suitable marinade) to put on the coals as the afternoon progresses. Make sure there is an ample supply of good bread.

Baba Ganoush

Serves 4

2 large aubergines
1 garlic clove, crushed
a scant ½ teaspoon salt
juice of ½ lemon
50g light tahini
60ml light olive oil
chopped fresh parsley or mint leaves,
to garnish

An aubergine-based recipe from the eastern Mediterranean, baba ganoush has a delicious slightly smoked flavour and is good as a dip, or as a side dish for barbecued vegetables or meat. I like the slight texture created by chopping the aubergine, but you can blitz it in a food processor if you prefer.

Cook the aubergines by grilling them over the barbecue (see page 126) or putting it directly over the flame of a gas hob. If using the latter, keep turning them, using tongs, until the skin is black and charred all over. (This makes a mess on the hob – put foil around the burner first if the idea bothers you. The aubergines can be cooked under a grill if there is no alternative, but a direct flame is better.)

Leave the aubergines to cool and pick the blackened skin off. Be careful, as they hold the heat from cooking for quite a long time, releasing very hot cooking juices from the middle. Once you have removed the skin, and the aubergines have cooled, squeeze the flesh over the sink to remove as much juice as possible.

Chop the flesh quite finely, then scrape it into a bowl and mix well with the garlic, salt, lemon juice and tahini. Add the olive oil and stir well again. Serve garnished with parsley.

Sheftali

Serves 4

1 lamb's caul

500g minced beef

a small bunch of parsley, leaves chopped

1 generous teaspoon salt

ground black pepper

good bread and Greek Cabbage Salad
(opposite), to serve

Simple but delicious, sheftali are a type of coarse sausage or kebab very popular in Cyprus. Lamb caul is essential — you will probably need to order this from a good traditional butcher. One caul should be ample for 4 sheftali, with a little bit left over.

Fill a large bowl with tepid water and put the caul in it. Unravel it gently so that you have a large sheet of transparent membrane with a lacy pattern of fat. Cut 4 roughly square pieces, each 15 x 15cm, avoiding any particularly fatty parts.

Mix the beef with the parsley, salt and pepper, then divide it into four portions. Roll up each portion in a piece of caul to give a neat, sausage-shaped parcel.

Cook over medium-hot charcoal, turning every few minutes. If the surface shows signs of overcooking, move aside to a gentler heat. The fat from the caul may drip onto the coals and ignite, so keep an eye on them. Sheftali need to be very well cooked: the caul fat melts and bastes the meat, and eventually the caul more or less disappears, at which point the sheftali should be done. This can take 30 miutes, maybe more. If in doubt, cut one open. It should be cooked all the way through. Serve with good bread and cabbage salad.

Greek Cabbage Salad

Serves 4–6, or more as part of a buffet

¼ hard white cabbage

2 tablespoons lemon juice

4–6 tablespoons olive oil, to taste

salt and coarsely ground black pepper

Simple and crunchy, this salad is a good accompaniment to burgers, steaks or sausages as well as sheftali.

Remove any tatty outer leaves and the hard central stem from the cabbage, then shred the remainder quite finely. Put in a serving bowl and dress with the lemon juice and oil, adding a little salt, and finish off with a scattering of black pepper.

Lime, Chilli and Coriander Butter

Makes about 325g

40g fresh coriander leaves

zest of 2 limes

juice of 1 lime

250g salted butter, cut into pieces

3 green bird's eye chillies, or to taste, deseeded and cut into small dice

This is good with vegetables such as sweet potato, sweetcorn and butternut squash, as well as seafood, fish and chicken.

Put the coriander, lime zest and juice into a blender and process briefly, then add the butter and blend well until well combined. Stir the chillies into the mixture and chill until needed, ideally overnight.

Cooking Vegetables on the Barbecue

All around the Mediterranean, people cook vegetables over hot coals, either as ingredients as part of a dish or to eat to accompany a meal. Mixed kebabs of vegetable pieces might look pretty but they are often disappointing – they cook at different rates so that the courgettes will be overdone while the onions are still crunchy. It's often better to cook them as separate items.

Asparagus Choose thick spears and snap off any very woody ends. Brush with oil and cook over medium/medium-low heat for 7–10 minutes until just tender, turning 2 or 3 times. Scatter with coarse salt before eating.

Aubergines Put whole aubergines over a high heat and use tongs to turn them until they are soft. The skin will char, which is fine. They can produce a lot of fluid in the process – this is scalding hot and drips onto the coals. Use tongs to lift them to one side and allow them to drain onto the ground. When they are soft all the way through allow them to cool to tepid, then peel off the skin, remove the stem end and use the flesh in Baba Ganoush (see page 122) or add to Barbecue Ratatouille (see page 129).

Butternut squash Peel, deseed and cut into 1.5cm cubes. Boil until just tender. Drain and toss in a little oil and lemon juice with a pinch of salt. Thread on kebab skewers with a small bay leaf between each piece and grill on the barbecue for 2 minutes a side or until cooked through. Thin slices cut from a chorizo sausage also go well in between the cubes of squash. Good with Lime, Chilli and Coriander Butter (see page 125).

Courgettes Cut large courgettes diagonally into 1cm slices and smaller ones in half lengthways. Toss them in oil and lemon juice, then grill on the barbecue over a medium heat, turning once or twice until tender. Serve as part of a vegetable selection to accompany meat or fish, or use in Courgette Salad (see page 135) or Barbecue Ratatouille (see page 129).

Mushrooms Use large flat mushrooms. Marinate with lemon juice and chopped herbs such as thyme and rosemary, then brush with olive oil and put them, gill-side up, over a fairly high heat. Turn after 3 minutes and cook until they are tender. Button mushrooms can be treated the same way, but thread them onto skewers before grilling.

Onions Peel small onions or shallots, then push them onto skewers and brush with oil. Grill on the barbecue for 10 minutes over medium-hot coals. Eat with grilled meat or in Barbecue Ratatouille (see page 129)

Tomatoes Thread small tomatoes onto skewers, or put larger ones directly on the barbecue grill. Turn frequently – they cook fast. Eat with grilled meat or fish, with Ravigote Butter (page 20) or in Barbecue Ratatouille (see page 129).

Peppers Put whole peppers over high heat and grill them on the barbecue until the skins begin to blacken and split. Keep turning them with tongs so that all the sides are done. Cool to tepid, then peel off the skins and remove the cores and seeds. Eat as part of a mixed vegetable selection, or use red peppers prepared this way in Sweet Pepper Relish (see page 148) or Barbecue Ratatouille (see page 129).

Potatoes These reheat well on barbecues. Cook new potatoes whole in boiling water until they are just tender, then drain and leave to cool. Cut them in half and marinate them in 2 tablespoons olive oil with the zest of ½ lemon and a little chopped fresh rosemary (they can be left for up to 48 hours in this, as long as they are kept cool). Thread onto skewers, brush with the oil remaining in the bowl, and grill on the barbecue until the cut surfaces are golden brown. Larger potatoes can be cooked the same way, but cut them into thick slices after boiling and put them directly onto the grill.

Sweetcorn Brush the corn cobs, without husks, with oil and put directly onto the barbecue grill. Keep turning until the kernels have developed golden-brown spots. Eat with butter, salt and smoked paprika, or Lime, Chilli and Coriander Butter (see page 125). For cooking sweetcorn with the husks on, see page 176.

Sweet potatoes Peel and cut into 1.5cm cubes, then boil gently until just tender. Drain and marinate in 1 tablespoon oil, 1 tablespoon vinegar, a little salt and a pinch of chilli powder. Thread onto skewers alternated with some cubes of halloumi cheese and grill on the barbecue for 2 minutes on each side.

Barbecue Ratatouille

Serves 4–6

1 aubergine

1 medium-large courgette, cut into 1cm horizontal slices

2 red peppers

4 large tomatoes

2 tablespoons olive oil

2 small onions, roughly chopped

1 small garlic bulb, cloves roughly chopped

salt

Barbecued vegetables make a delicious version of this Mediterranean classic, giving it an underlying slightly smoky flavour. Serve with plainly grilled meat – from sausages to steaks – and use good bread to mop it up, or cook some couscous or pasta separately to serve with it. The quantities of vegetables given here are approximate and depend to some extent on what's available, but aim for roughly even proportions of everything except garlic. The final step of mixing in a frying pan isn't essential – the onion and garlic can be oiled and cooked on the barbecue with everything else – but it helps the flavours to combine.

Using medium-hot coals, grill the aubergine, courgette, peppers and tomatoes over charcoal as described on pages 126–127. When cool enough to handle, remove the skins from the aubergine and tomatoes, and the skins and seeds from the peppers.

Heat the oil gently in a large frying pan over the barbecue. Fry the onions and garlic gently until soft. Dice the aubergine, cut the courgette into smaller strips, cut the pepper flesh into strips and cut the tomatoes into eighths. Add the barbecued vegetables to the pan. Stir well and cook gently for 5 minutes. Add salt to taste. Serve hot, warm or cold.

Alternatively, you can barbecue the whole onion and garlic in their skins, then remove the skins after cooking. Roughly chop the onion, garlic and all the vegetables as above, then drop them into a bowl, sprinkle with salt and drizzle with oil while they are still warm, mix well and serve.

KOFTA AND NAAN:
SOME INDIAN FOOD

———

The Indian sub-continent is another area in which people are masters at grilling and otherwise cooking over hot coals, often using improvised equipment. The grills range from tiny chula (little earthenware barbecues that use just a handful of charcoal) to enormous and blazing-hot ceramic tandoors. Although we are also-rans in comparison, there is no doubt that many of the Indian-derived recipes popular in the UK are good cooked over charcoal, and make great barbecue food, either alone or as an element of a larger spread.

Other items that are good with this menu are Baba Ganoush (see page 122), Avocado Salsa (see page 144), Chilled Cucumber Cream (see page 42) or a selection of grilled vegetables (see pages 126–127). For another meat course, try chicken portions treated with the rub recipe given on page 144, or Grilled Quail (see page 114). Add Spiced Rice Salad (see page 68) and Spiced Chickpea Flour Cake (see page 90) to give a larger selection. Serve a selection of summer fruit for dessert, or Fruit Salad in a Melon (see page 72) for a special occasion.

The Watermelon and Strawberry Cocktail (see page 137), the kofta mix (see page 132) and the naan bread dough (see page 134) can be prepared the day before and kept chilled, as can the Courgette Salad (see page 135) if the barbecue is lit; if not, make it before cooking the kofta and naan bread.

Lamb Kofta

Serves 4, with 2 large kebabs each

2 medium onions, peeled and roughly chopped

8 garlic cloves

2 thumb-sized pieces of fresh root ginger, peeled and roughly chopped

2 fresh green chillies, or to taste, deseeded

leaves of 8 fresh mint sprigs

2 tablespoons cumin seeds

1 tablespoon coriander seeds

the seeds from 8 cardamom pods

8 whole cloves

1 teaspoon black peppercorns

1 teaspoon ground cinnamon

2 generous teaspoons salt

cayenne pepper, to taste

2 medium potatoes, peeled (total weight about 400g)

800g minced lamb

oil, for brushing

I mould this mixture into long sausage shapes around skewers, but it can be made into burger-type patties if you prefer. It needs to be well seasoned with salt and chilli. Serve with a chopped salad of cucumber and tomato with a little chopped onion, naan (see page 134) or other flat bread, and some natural yogurt.

If this mixture is made up the day before, the potato should be added just before cooking. You will need 8 large skewers, or a grill basket designed for cooking patties.

Put the onion, garlic, ginger, chillies and mint in a blender or food processor and blend together to make a paste. Empty into a bowl large enough to hold the lamb.

Grind the whole spices in a spice grinder or using a mortar and pestle. Add this mix to the paste in the bowl and stir together with the ground cinnamon, salt and a dash of cayenne pepper. Put the lamb into the bowl with the spices and paste, and mix together well. This is best done with the hands, kneading well.

Grate the potatoes finely into a sieve and rinse well under cold water. Drain well, then turn out into a clean tea towel and wring hard to remove as much liquid as possible from them.

Stir in the potato and mix again, then chill the mixture for 1 hour.

Divide the mixture into 8. Wet your hands in cold water and shape each portion into a long sausage shape around a large skewer, or into a burger shape if you prefer. Brush them with oil.

Grill on the barbecue, starting with a high heat, and turning once when the side in contact with the grill is nicely brown. When the other side is well browned, move to medium heat until cooked through.

Naan Bread

Makes 8 small naan

1 teaspoon dried yeast

a pinch of sugar

500g strong plain bread flour, plus extra for dusting

100g natural yogurt

30g butter, plus extra for brushing

1 medium egg

½ teaspoon salt

Barbecues and the hot embers of open fires are excellent for cooking flatbreads, as long as there is a suitable metal surface such as a griddle, heavy frying pan or pizza tray that can be put over the heat. This is the best way for cooking naan bread without a tandoor. It is a good accompaniment to all sorts of barbecued meat, fish and dips.

Put 150ml tepid water in a small bowl and stir in the yeast and sugar, then leave to one side until frothy. Put the remaining ingredients into a food processor and add the yeast mixture. Process to make a softish, slightly sticky dough. (Alternatively, put the remaining ingredients in a large bowl, stir in the yeast mixture and mix well using a wooden spoon and your hands.)

Leave to rise in a warm place for 2 hours or until doubled in size – I sometimes leave this for 3–4 hours and it is fine. It can also be made last thing in the evening and stored in the fridge overnight, where it will rise slowly. Take it out for 1 hour before you want to cook.

When the barbecue is hot, knock back the dough and divide it into 8 pieces. Dust a work surface with flour and form each portion of dough into a cone shape. Flatten it for the characteristic tear-shaped naan bread, making each less than 1cm thick.

Heat a griddle or equivalent over hot coals. It should be very hot. Put 1 of the breads on the hot surface – it will start to puff up quite quickly. Press a spatula, or the flat side of a pair of tongs, down on it. Check the underside and turn after 60–90 seconds as soon as it looks golden in patches.

Cook the other side the same way, allowing a little longer for the heat to penetrate fully, then remove from the heat and brush over with a little melted butter. Wrap in a clean tea towel to keep warm while you cook the other breads in the same way.

Courgette Salad

Serves 4–6

½ small onion, sliced (optional)

1 garlic clove, crushed

1 mild green chilli, or more, to taste, deseeded and finely chopped

1 tablespoon white wine vinegar

3 tablespoons neutral oil such as sunflower oil, plus extra for brushing

1 tablespoon toasted sesame oil

1 teaspoon salt

4 courgettes

fresh coriander leaves, finely chopped, plus coriander sprigs to garnish

This is an invention born of numerous annual gluts of courgettes. Make it by cooking courgette slices directly on a barbecue grill. I prefer a seasoning mix that involves Asian flavours, but you can use a more European one based on olive oil, lemon juice and Mediterranean herbs if you prefer.

To make a dressing, put the onion, if using, in a serving bowl and add the garlic, chilli, vinegar, oils and salt. Stir well.

Cut the courgettes diagonally into pieces a little less than 1cm thick. Brush lightly with oil and cook over the hot coals until they soften a little and have grill marks. Add them to the dressing in the bowl as they become tender, and toss well.

(Alternatively, if the barbecue is not available, heat a ridged griddle pan and put the slices directly onto it, turning once they have grill marks on the side in contact with the pan.)

Add the coriander. Chill the salad if you don't want to use it immediately but bring it to room temperature before serving. Garnish with coriander sprigs.

Watermelon and Strawberry Cocktail

Serves 4

100g sugar
100ml water
4 large basil sprigs
1kg watermelon
500–600g strawberries, hulled
ice cubes, a few small, basil sprigs,
and extra strawberries or slivers of
watermelon (optional), to decorate

Make this lovely soft drink for sipping in high summer when strawberries and watermelon are plentiful.

Combine the sugar and water in a small saucepan over a medium heat. Stir until all the sugar has dissolved, then add 4 basil sprigs. Bring to the boil, then turn off the heat and leave to cool.

Cut the flesh from the watermelon and cut roughly into chunks. Put the melon and strawberries in a blender and process briefly, then push the mixture through a sieve to remove seeds and pips.

Discard the basil from the sugar syrup and stir the syrup into the watermelon mixture. Chill until needed and serve in glasses over ice. Decorate with a basil sprig and perhaps a whole strawberry or small sliver of melon.

SUNDAY ROAST ON THE BARBECUE

———

Here are two ideas for how to cook larger pieces of meat on the barbecue, one influenced by Australian and North American ways with chicken, and the other by Middle Eastern methods for lamb. Both require a kettle barbecue with ample space under the lid, and both meats take quite a long time to cook. Allow plenty of time, and have a supply of nibbles for guests to eat as the meat cooks. Although perfect outdoor food, it is probably best to try these recipes out in the comfort of the back garden, at least for the first time, so that a supply of kitchen implements is on hand for manoeuvring and cutting pieces of hot meat.

Knives, forks and plates are best for the chicken, and it is good accompanied by a selection of salads, or some grilled vegetables. In theory, at least, the lamb can be rolled in flatbreads and eaten with the fingers. Make sure there is a generous supply of paper napkins to hand.

The salsa mix is excellent alone as an appetiser salad with some bread or with any barbecued meat. Provide any other dips as desired, or serve a cold soup such as the Gazpacho Shots (see page 63) or Chilled Cucumber Cream (see page 42), with or without some finger food such as Bresaola Rolls (see page 56) or Lettuce Wraps with Chicken and Tongue (page 58). Alternatively, you could light up a small separate fire in a bucket barbecue or hibachi and grill some Prosciutto-wrapped Scallops (see page 116), or Marinated Barbecued Prawns (see page 163). While the coals are still hot, cook a vegetable selection to go with the chicken (see pages 126–127).

Spiced Barbecued Joint of Lamb

Serves 4 (if using shoulder) or 6 (if using leg of lamb)

1 teaspoon black peppercorns

½ teaspoon fennel seeds

a small piece cinnamon stick or ½ teaspoon ground cinnamon

1 teaspoon cumin seeds

freshly grated nutmeg

1½ teaspoons salt

1 tablespoon paprika

3 garlic cloves, crushed

juice of ½ lemon

3 tablespoons olive oil, plus extra for cooking

a half-shoulder of lamb (blade end) or fillet end of a leg of lamb, 1–1.5kg in weight

To serve

4–6 flatbreads, flour tortillas or pitta breads

Tahini Sauce (see opposite)

salad made with chopped tomatoes, cucumber and onion, and dressed with a little lemon juice and olive oil

chopped mint and coriander leaves

This is loosely based on the idea of shawarma, a Middle Eastern dish of lamb cut in thin slices, seasoned and packed on a vertical spit, which turns constantly in front of the heat. Very thin slices are shaved off as it cooks and are scattered over a flatbread. This is then dressed with salad and tahini, rolled tightly and wrapped in paper to be eaten in the hand. It is a difficult dish to replicate without the spit, but the interesting spice mixture and slowly cooked lamb are delicious. Although the leg of lamb is a neater, denser meat, it can be too lean and dry. Because of this, I prefer to use shoulder.

Put the peppercorns, fennel seeds, cinnamon stick and cumin in a small frying pan over a medium heat. Heat gently for 3 minutes, stirring constantly, or until they turn a shade darker in colour and release an appetising, slightly roasted aroma. Grind to a powder using a spice grinder or a mortar and pestle. Empty into a large bowl. Stir in a generous grating of nutmeg, the salt, paprika, garlic, lemon juice and oil to make a marinade.

If using shoulder, leave it in one piece. For leg, cut into the lamb where the meat is shallowest and remove the bone, making a piece of meat that opens out into a rough rectangle. Put the shoulder or leg in a large dish.

Add the marinade and rub it in well on all sides, and into any pockets or flaps left by removing the bone from the leg. Cover and leave in the fridge for at least 7 hours or up to 2 days, turning from time to time.

Light the barbecue. When the coals are covered with white ash and very hot, put on a pair of gauntlets and take a pair of long-handled tongs, or a poker or rake. Carefully move the coals out into a circle or two long lines, leaving space for a large foil tray to be inserted into the middle. Add about 600ml water to the foil tray. Put the grill rack back on.

Take the lamb out of the marinade and brush a little extra oil over the fat side of the leg of lamb. Put the lamb, fat-side down if using leg, on the grill over the foil tray, and close the lid. Check every 15–20 minutes, turning after about 45 minutes (although this may depend a little on the size of the piece of meat and the heat of the coals). Add more water to the drip tray if it starts to dry out. The lamb should be very well cooked and tender, and can take between 1½ –2 hours to cook.

Remove from the heat and leave to rest for 20 minutes, then carve into very thin slices. Meanwhile, warm the flatbreads through on the barbecue (don't let them toast and become rigid). Cut into one edge of the pitta breads, if using, to make a pocket. Allow everyone to fill their own flatbread or pitta bread: start with a layer of sliced lamb, sprinkle with a little tahini sauce, add a scatter of the tomato salad and a sprinkling of herbs. If using flatbreads, roll them up tightly around the filling before eating.

Tahini Sauce

Tahni — a paste made of ground sesame seeds — gives this light sauce a slightly nutty flavour. It works well with the Spiced Lamb (opposite) but equally with plainly grilled lamb or chicken.

Put the tahini in a small bowl and add the garlic, lemon juice, oil and parsley. Mix to make a stiffish paste, then stir in a little tepid water until the mixture is the consistency of thick cream. Add salt and pepper to taste.

Serves 4–6

2 tablespoons light tahini

1 garlic clove, crushed

juice of ½ lemon

1 generous teaspoon olive oil

2 tablespoons finely chopped fresh parsley leaves

salt and ground black pepper

Beer Can Chicken

Serves 4–6

1 large chicken

Seasoning Mix for Chicken (see page 144)

4–6 rosemary sprigs

1 small (330ml) can of beer. Cider, lemonade or even water will do the job just as well

This is an excellent method for cooking a whole bird on the barbecue, because it steams from the inside and roasts on the outside, producing moist, succulent meat and wonderfully crisp and well-flavoured skin. The original version, which begins 'open a can of beer and drink half of it' before going on to balance the chicken on the can, has a certain appeal, but variously specially designed stands and trays for 'beer-can chicken' are available. You will need a foil roasting tray, a large kettle barbecue with ample space between the lid and the grill, as the chicken has to sit vertically on the tray (I acquired a grill a couple of inches smaller in diameter than the one which came with the barbecue, so that it dropped further into the base).

Prepare the chicken by rubbing it all over with the seasoning mix, then leave it in the fridge for at least 2 and up to 24 hours. Light a charcoal fire with enough coals to grill for about 2 hours. Start with very hot coals.

When the coals are ready, put the rosemary sprigs inside the chicken. Empty about a third of the beer out of the can, then put it, still with the remaining beer inside, opened up, into the body cavity of the chicken. If you have a stand or tray, follow the manufacturer's instructions.

Move the coals (which should be very hot at this stage) out into a ring around the sides of the barbecue, and put a tray in the middle of the coals to catch any stray fat or juices. Put the grill rack back on, and on top of this put the chicken, sitting on its beer can tray, pushing the bird down well. Cover with the lid of the barbecue and leave to cook. Check occasionally to make sure the bird is still upright and is cooking evenly. It will take 1½–2 hours to cook fully. As a precaution, have some additional charcoal burning in a chimney starter or bucket barbecue to refresh the coals in the main fire if they seem to be dying down too much. When you think the bird is done, test the internal temperature of the meat using a digital probe thermometer; the minimum internal temperature should be 75°C.

Remove to a carving board, discarding the can, the rosemary and any liquid inside the bird. Leave the bird to rest for 15 minutes and then carve.

Seasoning Mix for Chicken

Use this seasoning mix for chicken pieces with the skin on or for whole birds. This recipe is sufficient for 6–8 chicken portions or 1 large chicken.

Serves 6–8

½ tablespoon black peppercorns

½ tablespoon cumin seeds

1 tablespoon salt

2 garlic cloves

zest of 1 lemon

2 tablespoons sunflower oil or light olive oil

1 teaspoon chopped fresh rosemary leaves

Put the peppercorns and cumin seeds in a dry frying pan over a medium heat and toast them for a few minutes until they turn a shade darker and give off a toasted aroma. Grind to a powder in a wet grinder or using a mortar and pestle.

Add the salt, garlic, lemon zest and oil, and process again, or use the pestle, to make a thick paste. Stir in the rosemary. Rub the mixture into the chicken at least 2 hours, or up to 24 hours, before you want to cook.

Avocado Salsa

This is a crowd pleaser and can be made 24 hours ahead. Eat it as a dip with vegetables or snacks, or with bread, as a salad, as a sauce with grilled meat or fish, as you please or just on its own, scooped guiltily from the bowl. The avocado must be fully ripe.

Makes about 450g

1 large beef tomato

1 large avocado

1 large garlic clove, or to taste, crushed

juice of 1 lime

1 green chilli, deseeded and finely chopped

1 small bunch of fresh coriander, leaves finely chopped, plus a few extra leaves to garnish

4–6 tablespoons olive oil, to taste

cayenne pepper or chilli powder (optional), to taste

salt and ground black pepper

Put the tomato in a heatproof bowl and pour boiling water over to cover, leave for 30 seconds, then drain and peel off the skin. Discard the core, seeds and surrounding pulp, and chop the flesh into 5mm cubes. Put them in a bowl.

Cut the avocado in half, remove the stone and scoop out the flesh with a tablespoon. Chop this into similar-sized cubes and add them to the tomato in the bowl. Add the garlic, lime juice, chilli and coriander. Stir in the olive oil, ½ teaspoon salt and a generous amount of black pepper. Taste and add more salt if you think it needs it, and adjust the chilli heat with cayenne if you like something spicier. Mix well, put in a serving bowl and garnish with coriander leaves. Chill until needed.

Barbecued Fruit Kebabs

Serves 4–6

½ a pineapple

2 bananas

3–4 apricots, cut in half and pitted, or
1 orange

60g caster sugar

2 tablespoons kirsch or rum (optional)

4 slices white bread, crusts removed

60g butter, melted

cream or ice cream, to serve (optional)

To finish off with, offer a barbecued dessert. These kebabs can be put together in advance for last-minute grilling. You may have to put a few more coals on to boost the heat, although they don't need high temperatures or long cooking. Fruits — some fruits, anyway — cook surprisingly well on a barbecue, and small pieces of bread make a deliciously crisp contrast.

Using a sharp knife, cut the top and bottom off the pineapple, then stand it on one end and cut off the peel and the 'eyes'. Cut the pineapple in quarters lengthways and cut out the core, then cut across to give slices about 1cm thick. Put the pineapple into a large bowl.

Cut the bananas into 1.5cm chunks and add to the bowl. Cut the apricot halves in half again, and add them to the bowl. If using an orange, using a sharp knife, cut a thin slice of peel and pith from each end of the orange. Put cut-side down on a plate and cut off the peel and pith in strips. Remove any remaining pith. Cut the orange into eighths and then into chunks and add them to the bowl.

Put 2 tablespoons of the caster sugar in the bowl with the fruit and add the kirsch, if using. Stir gently and leave to macerate for 30 minutes, or for up to 3 hours.

Soak 4–6 bamboo skewers in water for 30 minutes. Cut the bread into 1 x 2cm pieces. Lightly brush each piece all over with melted butter and then toss in the remaining sugar.

Make up skewers of the fruit, adding 2 pieces of bread to each kebab. Grill over medium or slightly cool coals until the bread develops crisp, golden-brown patches and the fruit is well heated and slightly cooked. Serve with cream or ice cream if you like.

CASUAL BARBECUE
FOR FAMILY AND FRIENDS

The food suggestions here are of the steak-and-burger nature and should cook easily and quite quickly. They are good candidates for packing up and taking out to a relaxing location with a view. A large bucket barbecue, or two, depending on the size of the party, should be all you need provided the coals are well managed – they should be medium-hot at the start. Or, if you're going to a campsite with barbecue pits, these foods are easily carried.

The Cypriot barbecue habits learnt by my husband's family have influenced this menu, so don't rush the burgers onto the grill as soon as the steaks are done. Take a relaxed approach to the meal on a sunny afternoon or warm summer evening. Spin out the event with drinks and nibbles, allow time for the children to skim stones or splash in the water, climb trees or examine the local insect life. Take a chimney starter to replenish the fire for a second round, cooking the burgers a little while after the steaks have been eaten.

Finish off with grilled peaches, or take some fresh fruit and a cheeseboard for dessert. Children might enjoy Baked Bananas (see page 200) as well.

Apart from the barbecue itself, refer to pages 107 and 110 about other equipment to take for cooking and cleaning and for ensuring you leave the embers properly extinguished before you leave. You'll need a nice board to portion the steak on, plates, knives and forks and napkins.

The various dips suggested elsewhere in this book go well in this plan, as do Avocado Salsa (see page 144) and Potato Salad (see page 41).

Sweet Pepper Relish

Serves 6–8

1 large tomato
4 anchovy fillets in oil
1 garlic clove, cut into slivers
4 pointed red peppers
3 tablespoons well-flavoured olive oil
salt

This evolved through my attempts to copy a Piedmontese dish of preserved peppers, and it makes a good accompaniment to barbecued meat, halfway between a dip and a salad. It's best eaten while the peppers are still warm, so prepare the other ingredients in advance and grill the peppers as soon as the barbecue is hot enough.

Put the tomato in a heatproof bowl and pour boiling water over to cover, leave for 30 seconds, then drain and peel off the skin. Cut the tomato in half and discard the core, seeds and surrounding pulp. Slice the flesh finely and put in a serving bowl. Cut the anchovy fillets into fine strips and add them to the bowl. Add the garlic and stir to combine.

Grill or barbecue the peppers until the skins begin to peel and blacken (see page 127). Allow them to cool a little, then peel off the skins and discard them along with the cores and seeds. Cut the flesh into thin slivers and add them to the tomato mixture. Add the olive oil, then taste and season with salt if needed.

Pissaladière

Makes 6–8 slices

1 teaspoon dried yeast

140g strong plain bread flour, plus extra
for dusting

40g butter, cut into pieces, plus extra for
greasing

1 medium egg

¼ teaspoon salt

For the filling

2 tablespoons olive oil

2 large onions, thinly sliced

2 large tomatoes

½ teaspoon salt

a generous pinch dried thyme

10–12 anchovy fillets in oil

10–12 black olives

The Provençal cousin of pizza, pissaladière is a mixture of very soft fried onions on a pastry base. It's good as an appetiser with drinks and is nicest on the day it is made.

Put 2 tablespoons warm water in a small bowl and stir in the yeast. Put the flour in a large bowl and add the butter, then rub the butter into the flour using your fingertips. Stir in the egg, salt and yeast mixture, and mix well to form a soft dough – add a little more water if necessary. (Alternatively, put the ingredients into a food processor and combine for 2 minutes.)

Put the dough in a greased bowl, cover with clingfilm and leave in a warm place to rise for 2 hours.

Meanwhile, to make the filling, heat the oil in a large frying pan over a medium heat and stir in the onions. Lower the heat and leave to cook very gently. Cover with a lid for the first 20–30 minutes, then continue to cook gently, uncovered, to evaporate the juices. This can take 1 hour or more. The onions should be very soft but still pale.

Put the tomatoes in a heatproof bowl and pour boiling water over to cover, leave for 30 seconds, then drain and peel off the skins. Cut the tomatoes in half and discard the core, seeds and surrounding pulp. Slice the flesh and add to the onions along with the salt and thyme. Cook more rapidly to boil off the tomato juice. The mixture should be moist but without much liquid in the pan. Turn off the heat.

Preheat the oven to 200°C and lightly grease a baking sheet. Knock back the dough then form it into a ball and pat it out with you hands to make a rectangle about 15 x 30cm. The yeast pastry will be quite thin. Transfer the pastry to the baking sheet.

Spread the onion mixture over the pastry, leaving a 1cm border all the way round. Gently level it off. Criss-cross the anchovies to make a pattern over the top and punctuate with the olives.

Bake for 15 minutes, then turn the heat down to 180°C and bake for a further 10–15 minutes until the pastry is golden and cooked underneath. Serve warm or cold. This is also good as a substantial snack on the beach or as part of a larger picnic.

Spiced Pork Patties

Serves 8

1kg minced pork

4 garlic cloves

long strips of lemon zest from 1 lemon,
cut with a vegetable peeler

12 juniper berries

2 eating apples, peeled and cored

1 teaspoon fennel seeds

2 teaspoons black peppercorns

a good pinch of cayenne pepper

8 rindless unsmoked streaky bacon
rashers, finely chopped

2 generous teaspoons salt

oil, for brushing

good bread rolls and coleslaw, to serve

These patties make for a tasty alternative to the more usual beefburgers: pork mixed with an Italian-inspired seasoning made with juniper berries, fennel seeds and fragrant lemon zest.

Put the pork in a bowl. Chop the garlic, lemon zest and juniper berries together and add to the bowl. Finely grate the eating apples. Crush the fennel seeds and peppercorns coarsely using a mortar and pestle (try to avoid reducing them to a powder). Mix everything together except the oil, then divide into eight and shape into rounds just over 1cm thick. Chill until needed.

Brush with oil and grill on the barbecue over a medium heat, turning once, until cooked through, making sure the meat in the middle is no longer pink. These flavoursome burgers work well with bread (see page 155) and coleslaw (see page 157).

Marinated Steaks

Marinade is sufficient for 1.5–2kg meat/serves 6–8

4 fresh bay leaves, spines removed and the green shredded, or 2 dried ones, crumbled

2 rosemary sprigs, leaves only, or 1 teaspoon dried rosemary

2 tablespoons fresh thyme leaves, or 2 teaspoons dried thyme

2 tablespoons fresh marjoram leaves or 2 teaspoons dried marjoram

1 lemon

300ml light olive oil

2 teaspoons black peppercorns, coarsely crushed

2 teaspoons salt

1.5–2kg rump steak, or other meat or poultry (see above right)

This marinade, based loosely around the herb mixtures of the northern Mediterranean shores, can be used for almost any food destined for the barbecue. Put it in a tray or box and add your chosen meat, fish or vegetables cut into suitably sized pieces. Leave for at least 2 hours, and preferably longer – up to 2 days. Turn the pieces in the marinade from time to time. It is especially good to season beef and pork, but it can be used for more or less any meat, fish or vegetable.

For a party of 8, buy at least 1.5–2kg of meat. I use rump steak and cut it into serving portions after cooking. As an alternative to beef, use pork steaks or loin chops (1 per person), lamb steaks or chops (1–2 per person, depending on size), or chicken breasts; the latter are best cut into two or three thick slices, for relatively fast cooking. All the above meats respond well to the marinade recipe.

If carrying the mixture to a location away from home, use plastic boxes or zip-type bags as containers to carry the marinated meat. Keep cool until you want to cook the food.

If using fresh herbs, chop the leaves coarsely, otherwise crumble the dry ones a little with your fingertips and put them into a small bowl. Cut the zest from the lemon into long strips using a vegetable peeler, then chop the lemon zest coarsely and add to the bowl. Squeeze out the lemon juice into the bowl.

Put the oil, crushed peppercorns and salt into the bowl and mix together well. Put the steak into a suitable-sized dish and pour over the marinade. Make sure the steak is completely covered with the marinade, then leave it for at least 2 hours.

When ready to barbecue, lift the steak out, allow it to drain and brush off any obvious pieces of herbs. Brush the steak with the liquid from the marinade in the early stages of grilling only (see page 111 about using marinades safely).

I prefer to cook rump steaks in relatively large pieces (cut a little on the thick side) to the desired stage of doneness, and then rest them for 10 minutes at the side of the grill, away from direct heat. I then transfer them to a board and cut them in slices to serve.

(Lamb can be cooked in a similar manner. Pork and chicken must both be well cooked – if in doubt, use a probe thermometer to check the internal temperature has reached 75°C.)

Burger Buns and
Bread Rolls for Barbecues

Makes 8 large buns or 16 slider
(small burger) buns

oil, for greasing

2 x quantities Bridge Roll dough (see
page 32), after the first rising

flour, for dusting

sesame seeds, for coating

1 medium egg, beaten, or milk or cream,
for glazing

*One can buy burger buns, of course; their bland softness is improved by toasting
them lightly over the coals before adding the meat. Or one can make them, in
which case the Bridge Roll dough (see page 32) makes a good basis.*

Preheat the oven to 220°C and grease 2 baking trays, 33 x 33cm square.
Divide the risen dough into 8 pieces. On a floured work surface, shape into
round buns about 6cm in diameter. Put the sesame seeds on a plate.

Brush the tops with egg and dip the top of each bun into the seeds. Put on
the prepared baking trays and leave in a warm place to rise until doubled in
size. Bake for 10 minutes or until golden brown. Remove from the oven and
cool wrapped in a clean tea towel to keep them soft.

These are best eaten on the day they are made, but they will keep reasonably
well in a tin for 24 hours. Split and toast on the barbecue grill if they are not
perfectly fresh.

Coleslaw in a Cabbage

Serves 6–8

1 handsome cabbage with some nice outside leaves firmly attached (Savoy is a good variety, or any well-hearted summer cabbage)

2 small-medium carrots, peeled and coarsely grated

1 small eating apple

1 tablespoon lemon juice

1 mild green chilli, deseeded and finely diced

1 tablespoon sunflower oil or other neutral oil

1 tablespoon black mustard seeds

1 teaspoon Dijon mustard

½ teaspoon salt, or to taste

30g full-fat natural yogurt

120g mayonnaise

chopped fresh parsley, to garnish

This dish requires a fresh, good-looking cabbage, free of any soil, of the type best obtained from someone who grows them. If the idea is too much, then just use half a small cabbage heart to make the coleslaw and put it in a pretty serving bowl instead. Choose your cabbage carefully. Examine it for dirt and residents — both are undesirable.

The proportions in the recipe depend on individual tastes and the size of cabbage available; they are intended for a medium one, but adjust according to taste.

Trim off tattered or unsightly outer leaves and wash the whole head of cabbage under running water. Submerge it in a large bowl of clean cold water and leave it to soak for 1 hour. Shake out the excess water, then allow it to drain very thoroughly, leaving it stem-side up overnight if possible.

Trim the cabbage stalk level so that it sits nicely on a flat surface. Part the outer leaves to expose the heart and slice off the top third, then carefully hollow out the heart, cutting the leaves away from the centre and leaving an outer rim 1.5–2cm wide. This is quite time-consuming and the stem is hard. A grapefruit knife is useful, but beware of using any knife forcefully. Mind your fingers, but keep carefully slicing and removing the leaves. The hardest part is the stem, which is best dealt with by making numerous cross cuts in all directions. Eventually, you will have a neat bowl-shaped hollow. Once you are happy with this, put it in the fridge to chill.

Take about a third of the heap of cut cabbage and shred it finely. Put it in a large bowl. Add the carrot to the cabbage. Quarter the apple and cut out the core. Grate the apple coarsely and put it in a small bowl. Add the lemon juice and mix the apple in well, then tip it into the bowl with the cabbage. Add the chilli. Put the oil and mustard seeds in a small frying pan over a medium-low heat and heat gently until the seeds turn slightly grey. Once they start to pop and jump out of the pan, cover and turn off the heat.

Put the mustard, salt and yogurt in a small bowl and mix well, then stir in the seeds, oil and mayonnaise. Stir well, then pour over the vegetable mixture and mix in until all is well coated. Put into the cabbage 'bowl' and sprinkle with a little parsley. Put the cabbage on a plate and chill well.

Grilled Peaches

Serves 8

8 peaches, cut in half and stones removed

8 branches of rosemary, stripped of leaves for most of their length (optional)

melted butter, for brushing

80g marzipan (optional)

cream or ice cream (optional), to serve

This is a good method for dealing with all those peaches sold as ripe, but which never are.

Preheat the grill. Thread two peach halves onto each rosemary branch or on a skewer so that the cut sides face the same way and brush all over with melted butter. Grill, cut-side down until the peaches begin to soften and cook.

Meanwhile, if using marzipan, divide it into 8 equal portions, then form into little discs. Put them on a small baking tray on the edge of the coals to warm through.

Add a piece of marzipan to the hollow of each peach half, then turn the peaches and put them skin-side down on the grill rack. As soon as the undersides of the fruit are cooked, remove them from the heat and serve with a little cream or ice cream if you like.

AT THE SEASIDE

If there is one outdoor location guaranteed to sharpen the appetite, it is the seaside. Beaches are also good locations for cooking on barbecues, providing it is permitted and you are not going to annoy other people with smoke or smells. This is another good opportunity to get out a bucket barbecue, although you probably won't be able to use one anywhere near a beach hut – the potential for fire is too great. Use a camp stove if you need to cook anything or boil a kettle in a hut. A friend always swears that sausages, fried on a camp stove and eaten hot-dog style with bread rolls are the best food for the beach. I'd take focaccia, to eat in the morning or at lunchtime, while it's still fresh.

Fish seems the logical choice to go on the barbecue, although it can be surprisingly difficult to buy good fish in seaside towns ('Take it with you', as Elizabeth David remarked briskly in one of her books). One might at least hope for freshly landed mackerel at some of the Cornish and south coast ports, or maybe even some that you've fished for yourself.

You'll need hot coals for fast grilling when cooking fish on the barbecue. Accompaniments are best kept simple. Try any of the dips and sauces given in this book, or Lime, Chilli and Coriander Butter (see page 125). I have fond memories of sardines eaten in beach cafés at Nazaré, north of Lisbon: they were simply grilled with a scatter of coarse salt to season them, and served with a salad of lettuce, slices cut crossways from enormous tomatoes, and chips. Should you happen across some freshly caught sardines, this is worth trying (buy the chips from a takeaway). Simple desserts are also good – Fruit Salad in a Melon (see page 72) or Grilled Peaches (see page 158).

Marinated Sea Bass

Serves 2–3

30ml white wine

30ml olive oil

½ teaspoon fennel seeds, lightly crushed

1 teaspoon coarse salt

1 teaspoon finely grated lemon zest

1 sea bass, about 400–450g, cleaned with the head and tail on

Skordalia (see page 28) and good bread, to serve

This is one of the best fish for cooking on a barbecue. I prefer to cook it without any wrapping because the skin crisps. Provided it is cooked carefully and not allowed to burn, this is delicious.

Put the wine, oil, fennel seeds, salt and lemon zest in a shallow dish big enough to hold the fish and mix well. Cut three shallow diagonal slashes down each side of the fish and turn it in the marinade, making sure some gets into the cuts and the cavity. Leave to marinate for 3–4 hours, turning occasionally. The coals need to be hot to medium hot.

Remove the fish from the marinade and put it in a wire fish basket. Grill for 20 minutes, turning several times and brushing occasionally with the marinade until cooked through. To grill the back of the fish, hold the basket on edge on the grill rack for a few minutes. Serve with Skordalia (see page 28), bread and a bottle of white wine. Beware of any bones.

Marinated Barbecued Prawns

Serves 4

8 large raw prawns, heads and shells
removed, tails on

2 tablespoons olive oil

1 tablespoon white wine

1 teaspoon finely grated lemon zest

a pinch of dried chilli flakes

½ teaspoon salt

Green Goddess Dip (see page 26),
to serve

These prawns are lovely as an appetiser or an element in a larger fish-based barbecue. The number of prawns per person really depends on how many you're prepared to buy. Two per person is about right if they are part of a mixed platter of appetisers. Single prawns, offered with the Green Goddess dip alongside, make a good hot canapé.

Take a small knife and make a shallow incision down the centre back of each prawn, then remove the dark vein, if present.

Put the remaining ingredients in a shallow bowl and mix well, then add the prawns. Leave to marinate for 2 hours. Soak 4 bamboo skewers for 30 minutes. The barbecue coals need to be hot to very hot.

Remove the prawns from the marinade, shaking off any bits, and thread two prawns onto each skewer. Grill for 2–3 minutes until pink, then turn and grill the other side until pink. Serve with the dip.

Mackerel

Serves 4

4 mackerel, cleaned with head and tail on
salt, lemon (optional) and good bread,
to serve

*Definitely one for the seaside, the key to good barbecued mackerel is the freshest
possible fish. Catch it yourself if you can. If not, try to buy it at the dockside or
from a fishmonger who has done so that day. The eyes of the fish are a good clue
to freshness: they should be bright and shiny, not sunken. The later in summer
it is, the fatter the fish will be. If you want to use a marinade, the teriyaki one
(below) is good with mackerel. Enjoy the fish with a glass of wine.*

You will need a wire fish basket.

The coals need to be hot. Put the mackerel in a wire fish basket and cook
over the barbecue for 8–12 minutes, turning occasionally, until cooked
through on the sides and backs.

Season with salt and a squeeze of lemon, if you like, and serve with bread.
Beware of bones.

Teriyaki Marinade

Serves 6–8

4 tablespoons light soy sauce

2 tablespoons sesame oil

2 tablespoons lime juice

2 tablespoons rice wine

a generous tablespoon clear honey

2 garlic cloves, crushed

2 x 2cm cube of fresh root ginger, peeled
and finely grated

6–8 mackerel, or fish or meat of your
choice

oil, for brushing

*A Japanese-style marinade, teriyaki is quite strongly flavoured and is good for
oily fish, including mackerel and tuna, as well as for beef, pork or chicken. The
recipe is enough to marinate 800g–1kg fish or meat.*

Put all the ingredients in a shallow dish and mix well together. If using
mackerel, make 3–4 diagonal cuts through the flesh of the fish on each
side. Put the fish or meat in the dish and coat it in the marinade. Marinate
for 30 minutes, turning twice. The barbecue coals need to be hot to
medium hot, depending on the food.

Remove from the marinade and shake off any excess. Brush the fish with
oil, put it in a wire fish basket and grill for 5–6 minutes on each side until
cooked. If using the marinade with meat, this can be cooked directly on
the grill rack.

Focaccia

Makes about 6 portion

1 teaspoon dried yeast

1 teaspoon sugar

200g strong white bread flour, plus extra
for dusting

150g Italian 00 flour

½ teaspoon salt

1 tablespoon olive oil, plus extra for
greasing

For the topping

for fried onion (optional): 1 large onion,
sliced, and 1 tablespoon olive oil

for herbs (optional): 1 tablespoon fresh
rosemary leaves or 1 teaspoon dried
rosemary, or 1 tablespoon torn sage
leaves or 1 teaspoon dried sage
5–6 tablespoons olive oil
½ tablespoon
coarse salt

Here is food for the beach, Italian style. Focaccia should be oily, salty and a little crunchy at the edges. It also needs to be fresh, so bake it on the day – although the dough can be made and frozen in advance, then defrosted overnight, rolled and baked to save time in the morning.

Put the yeast in a small bowl and add 150ml tepid water and the sugar. Leave to one side for a few minutes until it becomes frothy.

Put the flours in a bowl with the ½ teaspoon salt. Pour in the yeast mixture and add the oil. Mix well with a wooden spoon, then with your hand to make a dough. You may need to add more water; the dough needs to be a little on the soft side. Cover the bowl with clingfilm and leave for 10 minutes.

Uncover, then mix again for a moment, then recover. Repeat this process again, by which time you should have a nice, coherent springy ball of dough. Cover and leave for 1–2 hours until doubled in size.

Meanwhile, to make the topping, fry the onion, if using, in the oil for 10 minutes or until softened and golden. Leave to one side.

Preheat the oven to 240°C and grease a 30cm baking tray lightly with oil. Knock back the dough. Dust a work surface with flour and roll out the dough into a square to fit the baking tray. Put it on the tray, making sure it reaches the edges. Brush liberally with oil for the topping and scatter the coarse salt over. Add the onion, if using, rosemary or sage (or use all three, but in separate areas, not together). Then dimple the dough all over with the tips of your fingers. Leave to rise for about 30 minutes.

Bake for 12–15 minutes or until the edges are golden brown and crisp. Remove from the oven and brush with a little more oil.

Eat on the day of making, while warm if possible. It can be wrapped in foil and reheated gently over a warm barbecue.

TRAVELLING LIGHT

———

There is something appealing about impromptu snacks made with an element of improvisation and a minimum of fuss. They issue a challenge – how little does one actually need to cook a small amount of food? And what items – likely or otherwise – do you need to do this? Unless you're a bushcraft expert (in which case, naturally, you'll know how to make fire through friction using a couple of dry sticks) or a re-enactor (and so might be carrying flint and tinder), a box of matches or a cigarette lighter is essential. Apart from that, many useful fuel items and unlikely cooking materials can be gathered from the environment round about or abstracted from the recycling bin.

Likewise, a certain amount of food can be foraged from the environment (see also the section on Forager's Fare for more about this). Bear in mind that a little basic know-how can save a lot of grief. This goes especially for shellfish, of which mussels are often suggested as something to be collected off the rocks at low tide. If you are going to do this, be very careful about checking water quality in the area you are foraging in. Both sewage pollution and 'red tides' – algal blooms, which don't actually look red – can be serious problems and give nasty stomach upsets, especially in summer. It is less romantic but safer to acquire mussels from a fishmonger.

Some say that mussels should not be used when there isn't an 'R' in the month (that is, not from the end of April through to the beginning of September); this is partly to do with the higher chance of food poisoning in warmer months, and partly because it is the spawning season. It is a rule that seems to be ignored by many of our continental neighbours. However you have acquired them, the usual procedures apply: use mussels on the day that you obtain them; if you need to keep them, do so in a cool place, preferably the fridge, in a bowl; don't cover them or add tap water. When preparing, throw away any with cracked or broken shells and any open ones that don't close straight away when given a sharp tap. Just before cooking, pull off the beards (the straggly seaweedy part attached to one side of the shell). Once they are cooked, discard any mussels that haven't opened.

Here are two ideas for cooking mussels, and a few for other things, for when you're in a Famous Five mood, or dealing with trustworthy children who want a short adventure. They are a kind of minimalist campfire cookery.

Mussels Steamed in Seaweed

Serves 4

1.5kg fresh mussels, beards removed
a generous quantity of wet seaweed

Apart from the mussels you will need the wherewithal to light a fire that will provide a nice layer of embers, and some wet seaweed.

Light a fire on a patch of dryish sand or small shingle. Allow it to burn up for at least 30 minutes and make sure it leaves a good bed of small, hot embers. Cover these with a layer of wet seaweed (don't make this thick – seaweed holds the cold remarkably well).

Once the seaweed has warmed up a bit, add the mussels in a single layer, and cover them with a few more strands of seaweed. Leave until the mussels open, then eat them.

Éclade

Serves 4

1.5kg fresh mussels, beards removed
a generous quantity of dry pine needles
(long ones from true pine trees such as
Scots pine or its relatives)

In Charente-Maritime, an Atlantic province of central France, this method is used to cook mussels on beaches which have pine trees growing at the edge. It is worth foraging a bag of pine needles to take to the beach if (as in the UK) pine trees are unusual there. Apart from the mussels, you need a match or two, a sliver of wood to act as a taper and a patch of bare sand or small shingle, or a cast-iron griddle.

Lay out the prepared mussels in a single layer on your chosen spot or on the griddle. They don't have to be in a pattern, but it looks pretty if they are. Prop them so that the hinge end is pointing upwards. Cover them with pine needles to a depth of about 8cm.

Set fire to the pine needles (a taper is useful for making sure they catch well in two or three places, but once lit they should burn fast). Let all the needles burn, then winnow off the ash and eat the mussels straight from the shell. They are delicious.

In both of the above cases you might like to take some bread, some Lime, Chilli and Coriander Butter (see page 125) and perhaps a bottle of white wine, to be kept cool in a rock pool, of course.

Damper

Makes 4–6

250g plain flour
2 teaspoons baking powder
2 teaspoons salt
butter, to serve

You will need a zip-type bag, a campfire and 4–6 long narrow twigs of green wood, about 1m long, peeled of bark.

Damper is an Australian name for flour and water bread cooked over, or even in, the embers. Baking powder makes it lighter. It will never be the most elegant of breads, but it is fun to make. It should be eaten as soon as it is cooked, preferably with lots of butter.

Put the flour, baking powder and salt in a zip-type bag and take water separately – you will need about 150ml. When you arrive at your chosen site, pour the water into the dry ingredients, close the bag and knead the mixture well through the plastic. It should be very slightly on the dry side.

Divide into 4–6 pieces and roll each one out into a snake. Wind each piece around the narrow end of a long twig, pinching the ends well together so that the dough doesn't fall off.

Hold over the fire, turning frequently, until the damper has puffed up a little and is crisp and dappled golden-brown on the outside. Slide off the sticks and eat with butter.

Damper Dogs

Serves 4–6

4–6 small chorizo or frankfurter sausages

1 quantity damper dough (above)

tomato ketchup or mustard, to serve

Use the damper mix, above, to make impromptu hot dogs. You will need a campfire and 4–6 long, narrow twigs of green wood, roughly 1m long, peeled of bark at the narrow end.

If using chorizo, carefully push the narrow end of a twig lengthways through each one, then grill them gently for a few minutes over the embers to heat through. Wrap a snake of damper dough around each sausage, almost enclosing them, and proceed as detailed above, until the dough is cooked.

If using frankfurters, you will have to use the dough to keep the sausages in place at the end of the sticks. Wind it round the stick and sausage together and seal firmly. Cook the damper as before, turning frequently – this might be more difficult, because as the damper cooks the arrangement loosens a little and it may slide around. Serve with ketchup.

Fish Cooked in Newspaper

4 fillets of trout, mackerel or salmon
salt
bread and Skordalia (optional) (see page 28), to serve

Wet newspaper is more useful than you might think. You will need a piece of greaseproof paper per fillet, plus plenty of newspaper, a water supply, and hot embers on a barbecue or campfire.

Put each piece of fish on a square of greaseproof paper and sprinkle it with a little salt. Fold the paper to make a parcel. Take 6 sheets of newspaper, wet them, then wrap them neatly around one of the parcels; repeat with the remaining fish.

Arrange the parcels on the embers and allow the fish to steam for 20–30 minutes, depending on the thickness of the fish. Bread and perhaps a sauce, such as Skordalia (see page 28), go well with this.

Corn in the Husk

Serves 4

4 corn cobs with husk fully attached
butter and salt, or Lime, Chilli and
Coriander Butter (see page 125), to serve

Here is an excellent way of cooking sweetcorn. Make sure the corn cobs have the husk still fully attached covering the whole cob, not the ones where it has been cut off, exposing the end. The Lime, Chilli and Coriander Butter is delicious melted onto the grilled corn.

You will need a bucket of water, a few short lengths of string and hot embers from a barbecue or campfire.

Carefully peel back the husk, one leaf at a time, so that you can remove and discard the cornsilk (the fibrous threads that lie between the husk and the ear of corn). Then pull the leafy husk back over the corn. Tie the pointed end with string and soak the corn in water for 10 minutes.

Cook over a medium-hot heat for 15 minutes. Unfold the husk and serve with butter and salt to taste.

Potatoes in Tin Cans

Serves 4

4 small baking potatoes such as King Edwards

butter, for rubbing and to serve

salt

Using this campfire method you can cook baked potatoes without losing them in the embers.

You will need several empty food cans (400g size), a few small pieces of foil, and a campfire.

Rub the potatoes with butter and a little salt. Put one or two in each can, then cover the open ends tightly with foil. Stand the cans in warm embers and keep turning them. Test the potatoes after 35 minutes. When they are fully cooked, eat with more butter and salt.

Roast Chestnuts

Serves 4 as nibbles

200g fresh chestnuts in their shells

salt

Few smells are more evocative of a nip in the air than that of roast chestnuts. These are an autumn treat to cook on a campfire or the embers of a bonfire. In theory, you might be able to forage some sweet chestnuts (not horse chestnuts, which are inedible), or you can buy them from the market.

You will need a sharp knife and a campfire.

Using a sharp knife, cut a small slit in the shell of each nut and put them on a stone at the edge of the fire. Watch out in case they explode. After 15–20 minutes they should be cooked.

Pull them away from the fire with a stick or rake, and allow them to cool a little. When they are cool enough to handle, peel and eat with salt to taste.

Porridge in a Flask

Serves 1, generously

1000ml boiling water
8 rounded tablespoons jumbo oats
a pinch of salt
soft brown sugar and cream, or milk or golden syrup, to serve

After a night sleeping under canvas, you might not feel like foraging for dry wood to light your campfire. Helpfully, this recipe can be prepared the night before and makes for a hearty breakfast. For this easy way to make porridge, you will need a wide-mouthed flask with a 500ml capacity, plus a small saucepan or billycan and a spoon to stir.

The night before, pour 500ml boiling water into a nice clean flask. Let it stand for 5–10 minutes to heat thoroughly, then empty it out.

While the flask warms, put the oats, a pinch of salt, and about ¾ of the remaining hot water in a small saucepan or billycan. If possible, put this over the heat and bring just up to the boil. Pour this mixture into the heated flask, and add a little more water to top up if necessary. Stopper securely, and add the lid. Wrap the flask in a towel or sweater to help insulate it more.

The next morning, your flask should contain a generous helping of porridge, ready to eat. Stir it while it's still in there, then pour it out and eat with whatever you prefer – personally, I think anything but soft brown sugar and a generous spoonful of single cream is a waste of time with porridge.

A reasonable porridge can be made by putting the raw oats in the flask with the second lot of water, but it will never be as creamy.

(Provided you have a brush or a wooden spoon handle to wield the dishcloth with, cleaning out the flask is much easier than an ordinary porridge pan.)

FORAGER'S FARE

There are a few items that even the most inexperienced forager can't go wrong with. Blackberries should need no introduction to anyone: the most urban of urban dwellers should have encountered them along roadside fences, on waste ground or the edges of building sites, or even taking root in small back gardens. They provide late-summer fruit to eat with cream or ice cream, or to make into pies. Other reliable foraged foods include elderflowers, wild garlic and bilberries. The latter two require a trip to the right kinds of location, which, happily, are the kinds of places one might like to use as a base for camping or a walk. (For more detailed descriptions, and many more suggestions of plants to collect and use, see *Wild Food* by Jane Eastoe).

Bilberries (*Vaccinium myrtillus*), also known as blaeberries or whortleberries, grow on acid moorland soils, especially in Wales, the Welsh Marches and Derbyshire northwards. They form small bushes with tiny oval leaves that vary in colour from bright green to red, depending on the soil and the weather. The berries are ripe from early July to mid August, and are small and dark, sometimes with a pale-blue bloom. On sight, most people would recognise them as being similar to the cultivated blueberries widely available in shops (they are related). Picking large amounts needs patience, although they make worthwhile pies and jams, and an excellent summer pudding. Take a picnic, sunscreen and a hat, and be prepared to spend half a day on the moors and to come home with purple fingers. A handful can be gathered relatively fast, however, to go with ice cream, or with the thick pancakes on page 182.

Elderflowers from elder trees or bushes (*Sambucus nigra*) grow in hedges, on waste ground and squeeze into even the tiniest nooks and crannies of urban space. They bear masses of creamy-white flowers in umbels in June, with a pleasing musky perfume. Once picked, this quickly becomes less pleasant, so gather them just before needed, and don't carry them in a plastic bag, which also affects the flavour. Use them in the pancake recipe on page 184.

Wild garlic (*Allium ursinium*), also known as ransoms, grows in shady, damp woodland. The leaves appear around mid March. They are long, pointed, dark green and glossy, with a pungent, onion-garlic scent. In May they produce clusters of little star-shaped white flowers on the end of long stems with a triangular cross-section. There are a couple of plants that can be mistaken for wild garlic, so it's important to use a field guide if you are new to collecting them. A handful of leaves can be gathered in seconds, and will be sufficient for a dish for 2–4 people. Take only the amount you need. Wash it well, before use. The leaves can be stored for several days between layers of damp kitchen paper in a plastic box in the fridge.

Crempog

100g plain flour
45g caster sugar
a pinch of salt
160g full-fat natural yogurt
1 medium egg
butter or oil, for greasing
1 teaspoon baking powder
butter, syrup, sugar, berries, to serve

These are based on a Welsh recipe for a kind of small crumpet or pikelet, which I discovered while researching The Farmhouse Cookbook. *They are a little like American pancakes and are good with bacon, on their own with salty butter, or sweet, with some caster sugar and fruit.*

For camping, the batter can be made in advance and carried in a jar, jug, or zip-type bag. Take the baking powder separately and add just before cooking. You will need a frying pan or griddle plate, a tablespoon or ladle and a spatula – or at least, a knife you can slide under the cakes to turn them, and a heat source. A cup, small bowl or empty yogurt pot to mix the baking powder and water are helpful, though this could be done carefully in the bowl of a ladle or large spoon.

Put the flour in a bowl and add the sugar, salt, yogurt and egg, then beat to make a smooth batter – this can be using a blender at home, or take a bowl and do it by hand on site.

When ready to cook, heat a frying pan or griddle and grease it lightly. Combine the baking powder with 1 tablespoon water and immediately stir it into the pancake batter, mixing well.

Drop large tablespoonfuls, or small ladlefuls, of the batter onto the hot surface of the pan. They should spread a little (encourage this with the back of the spoon or ladle). Leave to cook gently until the undersides are golden brown and the tops are starting to develop small holes, then flip them over and cook until golden on the other side. Serve as soon as possible.

Ricotta and Elderflower Pancakes

Makes about 12 small pancakes

2 medium eggs

200g ricotta cheese

1 teaspoon finely grated lemon zest

2 tablespoons sugar

30g butter, melted

90g plain flour

a little brandy or grappa (optional)

about 6 heads of elderflowers, gathered just before cooking

sunflower oil or other neutral oil, for frying

caster or granulated sugar, and sliced strawberries (optional), to serve

Forage a few heads of elderflowers to make this delicious snack or dessert in early summer. The ricotta batter can be mixed 24–36 hours in advance and stored in a cool place (carry it in a zip-type bag for camping). The elderflowers must be picked and added at the last minute. When picking the flowers avoid those growing near roads or any that have insect infestations. A couple of teaspoons of brandy or grappa are a good addition to the batter but not always available in a camping situation.

I prefer to cook these in an ordinary frying pan with about 5mm oil in it – this gives a lovely crisp exterior to the cakes – but they can be made with a minimal amount of fat in a non-stick saucepan if you like. If the elderflowers are over, make the little pancakes without them and eat with strawberries, raspberries or blackberries.

Break the eggs into a bowl and add the ricotta, lemon zest, sugar and butter. Mix very well, then add the flour and stir again. Stir in the brandy, if using.

When you want to cook the pancakes, strip the flowers off the elderflower heads, trying not to get many of the little stalks into the mixture. Stir into the batter gently.

Pour enough oil into the frying pan to just cover the base, and heat carefully on a camping stove or fire. Drop in tablespoonfuls of the batter, flattening each one gently. Cook until golden brown underneath, then flip over and cook the other side until golden. Dredge with sugar, add a few strawberries, and eat hot.

For camping, the batter can be made up to 2 days in advance, provided it is kept cool. Carry in a zip-type bag and add the elderflowers just before cooking for best results.

Wild Garlic Omelette

a knob of butter
3–6 wild garlic leaves, depending on size
2 medium eggs
½ teaspoon salt
ground black pepper

There is something nice about the idea of gathering a few leaves and using them straight away, and this simple recipe makes the most of the garlic flavour. Bread is good for mopping up the juices, and if you want a more substantial meal, some smoked trout (see page 192) is a good accompaniment.

Melt the butter slowly in a frying pan. Tear the garlic leaves into shreds, then add to the pan and cook gently for 2 minutes or until they wilt. Beat the eggs with the salt and a little pepper and pour into the garlic and butter mixture to cook.

Serve immediately.

Wild Garlic Pesto

Makes about 130g

30g hazelnuts
25g wild garlic leaves
25g parsley
½ teaspoon salt
30g mature Cheddar cheese, finely grated
40ml extra virgin olive or rapeseed oil

Take some wild garlic leaves home and make this alternative to the more usual basil-based pesto. It is good with eggs, or with barbecued fish.

Preheat the oven to 160°C. Put the hazelnuts on a baking tray and toast in the oven for 10–15 minutes until pale gold, shaking the tray occasionally. Put the hazelnuts in a in a clean tea towel and rub off the skins.

Put the nuts, wild garlic leaves, parsley and salt in a blender and reduce to a paste. Add the cheese and blend again, then add the oil and blend until you have a thick, well-blended paste.

Fungi

Gathering fungi is an aspect of foraging beset with warnings of possible health risks, which must be taken seriously (my mother, a botanist and country dweller of long experience would have no truck with anything except field mushrooms). Try to go out collecting with an expert – look out for organised fungus forays, now held quite widely, and acquire a good field guide, such as Jane Eastoe's *Mushrooms*.

Once you feel confident over gathering wild fungi, late summer and autumn country walks take on a whole new purpose, in which anything white in a field has to be investigated in case it is a field mushroom, and the ground under the edges of woodland inspected for chanterelles and penny buns. Early morning is considered the best time for mushrooming, partly because fungi really do mushroom overnight, and partly because those in the know get out early before the competition.

Field mushrooms (*Agaricus campestris*), appear in August and September, and initially have domed white caps, which flatten and become creamier in colour with age. The gills underneath start out a pale pink, turning browner and ending up almost chocolate-coloured in older specimens (never eat anything with white gills unless you have expert identification, and do not eat anything resembling a field mushroom that develops a yellow stain when cut or broken). Field mushrooms are also much enjoyed by insect larvae, so remove the stem and examine the space it leaves on the cap for small holes.

The best use for a modest haul of field mushrooms is to fry them: make sure you have a supply of thinly sliced best bacon and cook this first until crisp. Keep it warm while the mushrooms fry in the bacon fat, and enjoy as a bacon and mushroom sandwich.

Chanterelles (*Cantharellus cibarius*) grow under trees, especially conifers or birch, in September and October. They are egg-yolk yellow and have trumpet-shaped caps with irregular wavy edges. The gills run from the edge of the cap almost all the way down the stem, tapering at the lower ends, and the fungi have a distinctive smell reminiscent of apricots. Chanterelles need to be carefully washed (soil tends to lodge in the gills). Slice or halve the fungi, depending on size, then fry them lightly in butter with a sliver of garlic. Finish by scrambling some eggs into the mixture.

Penny bun (*Boletus edulis*), describes something now better known in British gastronomy as ceps or porcini. The English name describes the appearance of these fungi: round golden-brown domes like freshly baked bread buns hidden amid the grass under trees. Instead of gills, they have tubes underneath, giving a sponge-like appearance. Beware of worm-eaten specimens and the related, but toxic, devil's boletus. Slice and fry in butter or olive oil, adding a little chopped parsley and garlic towards the end of cooking, or add to meat dishes.

AROUND THE CAMPFIRE

My childhood included numerous campfires, mostly belonging to other people. Curiously, no-one seemed to have heard of toasting marshmallows over the embers, though we often lost the jacket potatoes in the ashes. Many were lit by the troops of Girl Guides who camped annually in one of the fields of my parents' farm. Neatly organised, and protected from the rain by canvas awnings, they had heated, bucket-like pans hung over them, mostly, it seemed, containing baked beans or mashed potatoes. Relatives and family friends who sometimes camped on our land lit campfires too, for everything from boiling water for tea to fry-ups of bacon and mushrooms, or pots of potatoes and stews.

Later, life moved on to camping expeditions with primus stoves and people who insisted on dry mixes of the add-boiling-water-and-stir variety. Often, I wished I'd taken a supply of bacon and eggs along as well, as I knew there were other possibilities. This chapter gives a few ideas. Campfires are fun to build, cheering, and warming to sit round. Lit in shallow pits created by cutting out several pieces of turf, surrounded by a circle of flat stones, they link us to all those fires of time immemorial when humans depended on them for cooking the day's catch.

Ensure you have dry twigs and other wood – branches, small logs or chunks of bigger ones. As with barbecues, pine cones work well as firelighters: put a few in an egg box on top of a couple of sheets of crumpled newspaper. Cover with a handful of thin twigs and add a few thin branches. Set light to the newspaper. When the fire is burning up, add a couple more branches and a small log or two. Keep adding wood and letting it burn; once there is a good bed of glowing embers, allow the fire to die back and you're ready to cook. Balance pots and pans on stones beside the fire, and keep watch to make sure the contents cook evenly; or arrange a barbecue grill over the top to support them directly over the fire. When you're ready to leave, make certain the fire is out and replace any cut turf.

Onion Bombs

Makes 4–6

4 large onions, peeled

450–500g minced beef

a generous handful of breadcrumbs

4 tablespoons finely grated strong cheese, such as Parmesan or mature Cheddar cheese

4 tablespoons tomato ketchup

1 teaspoon salt

Potatoes in Tin Cans (see page 177) or boiled potatoes, to serve

Layers of onion make good containers for meat wrapped in layers of foil and baked in the embers. The Spiced Pork Patties (see page 152) also work well in this; omit the apple and bacon, and add some breadcrumbs.

Cut the onions in half from the top down to the root. Carefully scoop out the centres with a teaspoon, leaving shells 2–3 layers thick (about a third of this can be chopped into the filling recipe here, if liked; keep the rest to fry with sausages or add to another dish).

Mix the remaining ingredients together to make a paste. Divide the mixture among half the onion shells and top with the other half. Wrap each onion bomb in a double layer of foil. Twist the tops well to seal, then cook the bombs in fairly hot embers. Move them around from time to time so that they cook on each side.

Open one after 35 minutes and cut into it to test if it is done in the middle. If in doubt, re-seal and return to cook. They are best when the onion has browned a little underneath or in patches where the fire is hottest. Serve with potatoes.

Irish Stew

Serves 4–6

4 tablespoons olive oil

1 tablespoon Dijon mustard

1 tablespoon chopped fresh dill leaves

500g neck of lamb fillet, cut into small pieces

2 onions, roughly chopped

4 large potatoes, peeled and cut into chunks

salt

This recipe is to be cooked in a heavy casserole dish on the edge of a campfire. The marinade mixture can be also used for neck of lamb fillet for a simple barbecue as well as this stew.

Put the oil, mustard, dill and 1 teaspoon salt in a bowl and mix together. Add the meat, mix well and put in the base of a heavy flameproof casserole dish. Scatter the onions over the top. Leave to marinate in a cool place for 24–48 hours.

Put the potatoes over the meat and onions. Add water to come halfway up the level of the contents, and scatter a little more salt over the top. Cover the casserole and set on stones beside a campfire. Turn it round at intervals, and check a couple of times to make sure that it isn't drying up. It will need 1–1½ hours simmering.

If it's more convenient, the meat and marinade can be carried in a zip-type bag and the onions added at the same time as the potatoes.

Smoked Trout

Serves 4

120g salt

1 litre boiling water

4 trout, cleaned

oil, for greasing

Wild Garlic Pesto (see page 185) or salad, to serve

My favourite method for farmed trout is to hot-smoke it (this works for mackerel as well). It takes a while because, for the best flavour, the fish needs salting for a few hours (this can be done as in the Trout en Papillote recipe on page 195, or, for a better result, use brine as below).

You'll also need a barbecue with a lid and, crucially, wood to produce smoke. You can buy packs of chips of various wood species especially for using on the barbecue, or you could acquire some shavings or sawdust from a joiner. It is important that this is 100 per cent hardwood, and not softwood, MDF or any other synthetic material, and it should be free of solvents, glues, and so on.

For cooking the fish, it is best to have coals that are on the slow side; this gives the smoke time to penetrate the fish well and give a good flavour.

Make sure you are downwind of other people, and far enough away so as not to cause annoyance when the wood is added to the coals.

You will need 2 handfuls of small hardwood chips, such as oak, alder or apple, or wood shavings or sawdust. This is ample to smoke 4 fish. They are good hot or cold, so you might like to do extra for the next day.

Put the salt in a large bowl and add the water. Stir, then leave to cool. Take a deep tray or a large zip-type bag large enough to hold all the fish and the brine and pour the brine into it. Add the fish, then seal and leave in a cool place for 3–4 hours. Ideally, the fish will be submerged in the brine; if not, turn the bag every 30 minutes or so to ensure the fish is well soaked.

The barbecue coals should have been lit for some time and have burned down to medium heat (cook something else over them while they are really hot). Put the wood chips or wood shavings in water and allow them to soak for 20 minutes before using, or damp the sawdust well.

When the coals are ready, remove the fish from the brine and pat dry with kitchen paper. Brush with oil.

Use tongs to move the coals to the sides of the barbecue, leaving an empty space in the centre.

Drain the wood, shaking to get rid of as much water as possible, and scatter it over the coals. It should smoulder, not flare up and burn, and it will immediately produce lots of smoke.

Put the grilling rack in place, put the fish on it, and cover with the lid. Leave for at least 10 minutes, then check to see how well done the fish is. Cook for as long as necessary. Good hot with Wild Garlic Pesto (see page 185), or let the fish cool and eat with salad.

Trout en Papillote

Serves 4

4 trout, cleaned

3og butter, plus extra for greasing

1 tablespoon chopped fresh parsley

a few tarragon sprigs (optional)

1 lemon, thinly sliced

4 tablespoons white wine or cider

salt

bread, to serve

I leave the heads and tails on the fish, but this works equally well with fillets, and takes less time. If they have been salted before cooking, as in the previous recipe, there is no need to add any more during cooking. You will need to take lots of foil with you for cooking.

You will need medium-hot coals in the barbecue or embers of a campfire. Take 4 pieces of doubled foil, each large enough to enclose the fish well. Lightly grease the top layer of foil. Put a fish on each one.

Put the parsley, tarragon, if using, and butter in a bowl and add a teaspoon of salt. Mix together well then divide into 4 and put knobs of the mixture inside each fish. Put 2 lemon slices into each one, then pour a little wine or cider over them.

Fold the foil around each fish to make neat parcels and tightly roll the edges so that no liquid can escape.

Cook on the barbecue grill, or perch the parcels on embers raked to the edge of a campfire, for 7 minutes on each side. Open a parcel and probe against the backbone of the fish to make sure they are fully cooked. Open the parcels on plates to catch all cooking juices, and eat with bread.

Garlic Butter and Garlic Bread

Makes about 340g

40g fresh flat leaf parsley leaves

8 large garlic cloves, or to taste, roughly chopped

8cm celery stick from the heart, roughly chopped

2 teaspoons finely grated lemon zest

250g salted butter, cut into pieces

For garlic bread

1 baguette, cut in half if long

This butter is intended mostly for using in garlic bread, although it can also be used as a spread for sandwiches or as an accompaniment to barbecued food, especially chicken and salmon, or with mussels. Prepare ahead and store in a cooler, or make the garlic bread up to 24 hours in advance and wrap it up for heating as needed.

Put the parsley in a bowl and pour over enough boiling water to cover. Drain immediately and refresh in cold water. Squeeze dry in kitchen paper.

Put the parsley and the remaining ingredients in a food processor and whizz to a smooth paste.

If making garlic bread, preheat the oven, if using, to 220°C. Take the baguette and cut it into 1cm diagonal slices, not quite through to the base. Spread the side of each slice with the soft garlic butter, then wrap the baguette, or each half separately, in foil. Heat through in the oven, or on a barbecue or beside a campfire for 20 minutes until warmed through and the butter is completely melted.

Magic Pudding Baked in Orange Skins

Serves 4 greedy people, or 8 less
hungry ones

50g plain flour
¼ teaspoon baking powder
¼ teaspoon salt
2 tablespoons unsweetened cocoa
powder
100g caster sugar
90g butter, melted
1 medium egg, beaten
½ teaspoon vanilla extract
8 medium-large oranges

For the sauce
40g soft brown sugar
3 tablespoons unsweetened cocoa
powder
8 tablespoons boiling water

A magic pudding is a chocolate mix sprinkled with cocoa and sugar, with hot water poured over the top before baking. The water percolates down during cooking to make a sauce underneath the cake layer.

Cooking in the orange skins means you can enjoy baking on the move, and the orange gives a lovely flavour to the pudding.

You will need a generous amount of foil for wrapping the puddings.

Put the flour in a large bowl and add the baking powder, salt, cocoa and sugar. Stir together well. Stir in the butter, egg and vanilla. To make the sauce, put the brown sugar and cocoa in a bowl and stir together.

Cut a lid from each orange about one-quarter to one-third of the way down. Holding the orange over a bowl, carefully scoop out the flesh into the bowl, being careful not to break the orange skins. (Use the fresh orange juice and segments for breakfast.)

Divide the cake mixture among the orange skins. Don't overfill them – the mixture needs to be just below the halfway mark. Scatter some of the brown sugar and cocoa mixture on top.

Just before you are ready to cook, add 1 tablespoon boiling water to each orange. Put the 'lids' back on top and wrap each orange in a double layer of foil. The mixture expands as it cooks and may boil out at the top if the coals are hot.

Put the parcels in the warm ashes of a campfire or over low embers on a barbecue. They will need about 30 minutes to cook. Move them around occasionally so that they are evenly heated.

Unwrap and eat with a spoon directly from the shell. Be careful, as the pudding is very hot when taken straight from the fire.

Baked Banana

Serves 1

1 ripe banana in its skin
2 squares of chocolate
double cream or ice cream (optional),
to serve

Bananas baked in their skins make good barbecue or campfire desserts, especially loved by children. Chocolate is the simplest addition, or you could use the brown sugar mix below. Vanilla ice cream goes well with this if you have it available, or try a little cold double cream instead.

If cooking on the barbecue. Put the banana on the grill rack. Cook until the skin discolours and browns or turns black, depending on how well you like it done. Turn using tongs to make sure both sides are done. Over a medium heat it will take about 20 minutes to cook through.

If cooking on a campfire, wrap the banana in foil and bury it in the hot ashes of the campfire for a similar length of time.

Remove the banana from the heat and put on a serving dish. Cut a slit in the skin of the banana, insert the chocolate, and give it 2 minutes to melt before eating. Open the skin and serve with a little cream or ice cream, if you like.

Brown Sugar Mixture for Baked Banana

Serves 1

1 ripe banana in its skin
2 teaspoons soft light brown sugar
2 teaspoons butter
2 teaspoons rum

Adults might prefer this combination, with rum and brown sugar.

Slit the banana skin along its length. Add the sugar and butter to the opening and pour over the rum. Cook the bananas as for Baked Banana, above, and eat hot.

Hot Buttered Rum

Serves 1

25ml rum
25ml boiling water
1 teaspoon soft brown sugar
1 knob of butter the size of a hazelnut
a squeeze of orange juice
freshly grated nutmeg

Rich and indulgent, this is the perfect drink to warm you on chilly nights spent under canvas or otherwise outdoors.

Put the rum in a small heatproof cup, mug or a warmed glass. Add the boiling water and stir in the sugar. Float the butter on top, squeeze in the orange juice and grate a little nutmeg over the drink.

Conversion Table

WEIGHTS

7.5g	¼ oz
15g	½ oz
20g	¾ oz
30g	1oz
35g	1¼ oz
40g	1½ oz
50g	1¾ oz
55g	2oz
60g	2¼ oz
70g	2½ oz
80g	2¾ oz
85g	3oz
90g	3¼ oz
100g	3½ oz
115g	4oz
125g	4½ oz
140g	5oz
150g	5½ oz
170g	6oz
185g	6½ oz
200g	7oz
225g	8oz
250g	9oz
285g	10oz
300g	10½ oz
310g	11oz
340g	12oz
370g	13oz
400g	14oz
425g	15oz
450g	1lb
500g	1lb 2oz
565g	1¼ lb
680g	1½ lb
700g	1lb 9oz
750g	1lb 10oz
800g	1¾ lb
900g	2lb
1kg	2lb 3oz
1.1kg	2lb 7oz
1.4kg	3lb
1.5kg	3½ lb
1.8kg	4lb
2kg	4½ lb
2.3kg	5lb
2.7kg	6lb
3.1kg	7lb
3.6kg	8lb
4.5kg	10lb

OVEN TEMPERATURES

	FAN	CONVENTIONAL	GAS
Very cool	100°C	110°C/225°F	Gas ¼
Very cool	120°C	130°C/250°F	Gas ½
Cool	130°C	140°C/275°F	Gas 1
Slow	140°C	150°C/300°F	Gas 2
Moderately slow	160°C	170°C/325°F	Gas 3
Moderate	170°C	180°C/350°F	Gas 4
Moderately hot	180°C	190°C/375°F	Gas 5
Hot	190°C	200°C/400°F	Gas 6
Very hot	200°C	220°C/425°F	Gas 7
Very hot	220°C	230°C/450°F	Gas 8
Hottest	230°C	240°C/475°F	Gas 9

VOLUME

5ml	1 teaspoon	
10ml	1 dessertspoon	
15ml	1 tablespoon	
30ml	1fl oz	
40ml	1½ fl oz	
55ml	2fl oz	
70ml	2½ fl oz	
85ml	3fl oz	
100ml	3½ fl oz	
120ml	4fl oz	
130ml	4½ fl oz	
150ml	5fl oz	
170ml	6fl oz	
185ml	6½ fl oz	
200ml	7fl oz	
225ml	8fl oz	
250ml	9fl oz	
270ml	9½ fl oz	
285ml	10fl oz	½ pint
300ml	10½ fl oz	
345ml	12fl oz	
400ml	14fl oz	
425ml	15fl oz	¾ pint
450ml	16fl oz	
465ml	16½ fl oz	
565ml	20fl oz	1 pint
700ml	25fl oz	1¼ pints
750ml	26fl oz	
850ml	30fl oz	1½ pints
1 litre	35fl oz	1¾ pints
1.5 litres	53fl oz	2½ pints

LENGTH

5mm	¼ in
1cm	½ in
2cm	¾ in
2.5cm	1in
6cm	2½ in
7cm	2¾ in
7.5cm	3in
9cm	3½ in
10cm	4in
18cm	7in
20cm	8in
22cm	8½ in
23cm	9in
25cm	10in
27cm	11in
30cm	12in
35cm	14in
38cm	15in

Index

Further Reading

Georgina Battiscombe, *English Picnics*, The Country Book Club, 1951
Annie Bell, *The Camping Cookbook*, Kyle Books, 2010
Annie Bell, *The Picnic Cookbook*, Kyle Books, 2012
Jonathan Deutsch and Megan J. Ellis, *Barbecue: A Global History*, Reaktion Books, 2014
Martin Dorey, *The Camper Van Cookbook*, Salt Yard Book Co., 2010
Jane Eastoe, *Mushrooms*, National Trust, 2008
Jane Eastoe, *Wild Food*, National Trust, 2008
Laura Mason, *Good Old Fashioned Roasts*, National Trust, 2009
Laura Mason, *Farmhouse Cookbook*, National Trust, 2009
Stéphane Reynaud, *Stéphane Reynaud's Barbecue*, Murdoch Books, 2011
Claudia Roden, *Picnics and Other Outdoor Feasts*, Grub Street, 2012

The Weber Barbecue site is full of good tips on managing the coals and cooking:
www.weberbbq.co.uk

For more information on where to eat outdoors and the countryside code visit Nature England:
https://www.gov.uk/government/publications/the-countryside-code

If fishing, please ensure this is done responsibly. Check if fishing is allowed in the area and ensure you have appropriate licenses if required.

For more information on National Trust properties and events, please visit:
www.nationaltrust.org.uk

Acknowledgements

Many people provided ideas and help, including Sarah Barber, Valerie Berry, Erin Dodd, Stella Hobbs, Alex Krook, Janalice Merry, Elisabeth Orsini, Nuray Ösaslan, Jean and Roger Pinder, Brendon Stewart and Marylou Sturgeon. Thanks to Justin and Alison Sturgeon for lending me their large kettle barbecue; to Kurt Bauwens, who told me how to cook an 80lb pig, even if this didn't get into the book, and to Sally Nalle, who taught me about pine cones; to Paul and Barbara Chesmore for allowing me to light a campfire in their back garden; to Jean and Kerrich Hartshorne, and to Pam Hartshorne for the use of Bells' View, Kippford; and to Lucy Smith for editorial help. I owe a debt to Claudia Roden's book *Picnics and Other Outdoor Feasts*, and to the work of early and mid 20th-century writers such as Mrs Leyel and Ambrose Heath. Most of all, thanks to Derek, for much barbecue know-how and patience.

Senior Commissioning Editor: Peter Taylor
Project Editor: Lucy Smith
Designer: Lee-May Lim
Photographer: Yuki Sugiura
Home Economist: Valerie Berry
Stylist: Wei Tang